Praise for CURATING A WORLD

Rev. Neichelle Guidry is a burgeoning voice amongst millennial preachers. I have watched her development over the past several years. Over this time, I have heard her undeniably anointed voice become increasingly and distinctly prophetic. Her keen biblical insights, coupled with timely analysis of national and global events and her commitment to her own authenticity, make for a stirring presentation of fresh homiletical air.

—Martha Simmons

* * *

Rev. Neichelle Guidry is a leader, a gatherer, and someone who is deeply committed to fulfilling her purpose in Christ and inspiring others to do the same. It was an honor to have her close out the 2015 Justice Conference in Chicago. She did so with deep passion, conviction, and fire; united with a call to put Jesus first, to discover and walk in the calling He has given, and to be engaged in world around us. *curating a world* challenges us to dig deep and embrace what God has in store for us.

—Mark Reddy, Executive Director
The Justice Conference

* * *

curating a world offers up the homiletical genius of a shining leader among millennial preachers in the nation. Guidry's prophetic theological imagination gracefully weaves themes of redemptive love, justice, and liberation through proclamation that dances Good News from every page. The book is a womanist preaching masterpiece that accompanies Guidry's visionary ministry to the church and the world!

—Rev. Eboni Marshall Turman, PhD
Assistant Research Professor, Theological Ethics and Black Church Studies;
Director, Office of Black Church Studies
Duke University Divinity School

Neichelle Guidry knows how to preach because she knows how to listen – to her own truth, to the realities of the world around her, and to the voice of God speaking in our day. She preaches with power and passion, as well as humility and compassion, meeting us in our brokenness as she dares to name her own. Hers is not a solo act, but a generous recognition of herself as a member of a community of preachers, as she issues a call to her millennial sisters to speak their own truth. She's not about old-time exhortation, but new-day invitation, a powerful invitation to discover God right in the middle of our world and your life, and begin to shape a new world of love and justice. Answer her invitation, and you just may discover your own call to live into your deepest self, and thus into the heart of God.

—THE REVEREND ANNE HOWARD
Preacher-in-Residence, Trinity Episcopal Church, Santa Barbara, CA
Author of *Claiming the Beatitudes*

* * *

The Rev. Neichelle Guidry is a woman after God's own heart. Anyone who has ever heard her preach knows that she is not only called, but extremely gifted to communicate the love, grace and passion of God with a life with God. She is a woman who has seriously contemplated her life, her relationships, her community, and the world; and has come to understand that all are connected. *curating a world* is meant invite people to live and live abundantly. All who encounter her faithful words and are seeking a message of justice, hope and love will not be disappointed. As a model for living an integrated life, Rev. Neichelle beautifully invites us all to join a journey that leads to a deepening of faith and expansion of our understanding of who God is and what God desires for all of humanity.

—ROZELLA HAYDÉE WHITE, M.A.R.
Writer, Teacher, Coach and Consultant
Director, Young Adult Ministry for the Evangelical Lutheran Church in America

* * *

Guidry's poetic and prophetic collection of sermonic works breathes life into a valley of dry bones and invites all to share in the manifestation of God's Beloved Community. She preaches with creative, intentional and unapologetic vigor "for such a time as this," offering rich homiletic expositions of love and hope that we can all believe and curate together.

—REV. WALTRINA N. MIDDLETON, CLEVELAND ACTION
Freedom Poet, Community Rouser, Minister and Social Critic

CURATING A WORLD
SERMONIC
WORDS FROM A YOUNG WOMAN
WHO PREACHES

REV. NEICHELLE R. GUIDRY
FOREWORD BY DR. OTIS MOSS III

MMGI BOOKS • CHICAGO

Published by MMGI Books, Chicago, IL 60636
www.mmgibooks.com

Curating A World: Sermonic Words from a Young Woman who Preaches
Copyright © 2016 by Neichelle R. Guidry
All rights reserved.

Except for brief quotations used in reviews, articles, or other media, no part of this book may be reproduced or transmitted in any form or by any means, electronic or mechanical, including photocopying, recording, or by information storage or retrieval system, without permission by the publisher.

Except for quotations from Scripture, the quoted ideas expressed in the book are not, in all cases, exact quotations, as some have been edited for clarity and brevity. In all cases, the author has attempted to maintain the speaker's original intent. In some cases, quoted material for this book was obtained from secondary sources, primarily print media. While every effort was made to ensure the accuracy of these sources, the accuracy cannot be guaranteed.

Library of congress Cataloging-in-Publication Data
Curating A World: Sermonic Words from a Young Woman who Preaches
Guidry, Neichelle R.
p. cm
ISBN 978-1-939774-22-4 (pbk. :alk. Paper)
Religious life. 2. Conduct of life. 3. Christian Education.

Scriptures marked NIV are from the Holy Bible, New International Version, Copyright © 1973, 1978, 1984 by International Bible Society. Used by permission of Zondervan Publishing House. All rights reserved.

Bible quotations in this volume are from The Holy Bible, King James Version (KJV). Used by permission. All rights reserved.

Scripture quotations marked NRSV are taken from the New Revised Standard Version of the Bible, copyright © 1989, by the Division of Christian Education of the National Council of Churches of Christ in the United States of America and are used by permission. All rights reserved.

Printed in the U.S.A.

CONTENTS

Acknowledgments vii
Foreword *by Rev. Dr. Otis Moss III* ix
Preface xi

PART I: WOMAN WORDS 1
I'm In a New Place 3
What About Your Bones? 13
If Justice Were a Woman 26
Handing Our Baggage to God: 33
    Restoring the Dance of our Daughters
I Have a Question 43

PART II: JUST WORDS 51
Jesus Is Still at The Table 53
Don't Miss the Kingdom 63
Public Displays of Affection 77
Here I am to Worship 82
Live Into the Crown 90

PART III: LIBERATING WORDS 99
When the Water Calls 101
Go Get Your Joy 112
The Anatomy of a Testimony 120
It's Time to Get Excited 127
What I Know for Sure 136

About the Author 145

ACKNOWLEDGMENTS

This book has been a long time in the making, and it has come to fruition with the help and encouragement of many.

First, I want to thank my family. When I answered my call to ministry almost fifteen years ago, they were the first to affirm my gifts and to support my voice. To my parents, I thank you for always being willing to invest in my growth and development. You have always believed in me, even when I have taken risks. To my brother and my sister, thank you for your presence and support. The two of you are my completing parts. After having grown up together, I realize that there is no one who can take your place in my life. To my niece and nephews, Auntie loves you very much! I hope that you know that there's nothing that you can't accomplish in this world. I am deeply grateful to each of you.

I am grateful to my two best friends, Porscha and Brittany. Thank you for being my sisters. Thank you for holding me accountable for my dreams and for supporting my vision for my life.

I want to thank two congregations. I am deeply grateful to the family of New Creation Christian Fellowship of San Antonio, Texas. You raised me in the things of God and taught me how to walk with Christ. You saw the call of God in me before I saw it in myself. Bishop and Pastor Copeland, you were my first pastors. For years, through your examples, you showed me what it means to be excellent in ministry. Thank you for your love. I am also grateful to the village of Trinity United Church of Christ of Chicago, Illinois. For the past several years, you have been my Chi-town family. I truly believe that "love" is an understatement for how I feel about you. I am indebted to you for your support, not only of my ministry, but also of my entire life. Your prayers have carried me through all of the growth and changes of the past several years. It is an honor and a pleasure to serve you. In particular, I thank Rev. Linda Mootry-Dodd for being my advocate. I also thank my pastor and my brother, Rev. Dr. Otis Moss III, for the many ways you have supported, inspired and shaped my ministry. It is humbling to serve with you and to learn from you.

Finally, I want to dedicate this volume to my grandparents, the late Rev. Alvin Evans, Sr. and Mrs. Vivian Evans. You never missed a birthday or a graduation. I owe you everything. I know that I am a product of your prayers. I consider it my mission to make you proud, and to continue to do what you charged to do many years ago: make Jesus famous.

January 2016

FOREWORD

The preaching experience is a mystic art. The preacher is compelled to bring the fullness of her being to the act, intellect, drama, humor, song, insecurity, creativity, spirituality, theology, history, and a dash of swagger.

Historically, the preacher in America has been revered and reviled. Revered, when prophetic rhetoric bumps up against the stain of false democracy and a new portrait of America is rendered through prophetic speech. Reviled, when obvious divine gifts are leased to human hubris and market-driven concerns of personal wealth and enrichment take over. The preacher, no matter how committed, is forced to confront and answer for the worse of the tradition.

One of the joys of pastoring is to have the opportunity to witness greatness in its infancy. The gift of watching a person obviously gifted by God, who stands in the river of the best our tradition and is unafraid to stare down those who stain the sacred work with an irrelevant and personal gospel. Rev. Neichelle Guidry is one such preacher, standing in the sunrise of her vocation.

It was the former professor at Yale Divinity School, and now Dean at Vanderbilt Divinity School, Emilie Townes, who connected me with Neichelle during a visit to New Haven, CT in 2009. I was moved by this young seminarian's deep commitment to justice and joyous love of Black music (not just Gospel or Hip-Hop), but a broad understanding of the theological dimensions of Black music as an organic vehicle to transmit culture and stories of resistance.

Since joining the Village of Trinity, I have watched this gifted woman of God engage the #BlackLivesMatter movement, create an online space for women in ministry, called *shepreaches.com*, and of course, preach with intellectual honesty and pure Pentecostal fire to the people of Trinity United Church of Christ.

Rev. Guidry's preaching gift is connected at the nexus of Pentecostalism and academic curiosity, while shaped by her generational connectivity to resistance styled Hip-Hop. This contribution is spiritually ferocious and simultaneously, intergenerational. One can hear the influence in her preaching of her pastor, Dr. Claudette Copeland, one of our greatest proclaimers of the Gospel. Coupled with a beautiful Southern pathos in her speech, she walks the wonderful and difficult path of being a connector. What do I mean by this? Rev. Guidry is Southern, yet versed in Northern culture. Rev. Guidry is Pentecostal yet serving a United Church of Christ community. Rev. Guidry is a proud HBCU graduate, but familiar with the Ivy League culture of Yale University. Rev. Guidry is Afro-centric, yet connected to the cultural narratives of the global indigenous communities. Rev. Guidry is a Womanist committed to the liberation of broken people, and also a classic proclaimer of the Gospel of Jesus Christ.

I invite you to not only read these messages, but to also get your hands on an audio or video of these presentations. A true Rev. Guidry message must not just be read, but experienced. It is my hope that this wonderful preacher who has become a sister and friend to our family and wider village known as Trinity United Church of Christ will bless you.

Rev. Dr. Otis Moss III
Senior Pastor, Trinity United Church of Christ
Chicago, IL

PREFACE

On a random day in 2015, I found myself backed into a corner. The center of my world was crumbling, and I knew that I had to start over. I was stuck. I had been for almost four years, and two therapists had confirmed this to me on more than one occasion. I was in a bad situation, and I needed to do something about it.

I believe that in any situation that God doesn't intend for us, God sends moments of utter clarity. These are critical moments in which one has to decide what she's going to do and how she will enact her agency. Call it prophetic timing, God-moments, or "straws that break the camel's back." Whatever you call it, the purpose is the same. These moments come to push us, to urge us from within, to call our attention to how powerless we've allowed our circumstances to render us. And if one is discerning and courageous enough, she responds, with all fear, all heart and all spirit, trusting that no matter the outcome, what is ahead of her is surely better than what she has left behind. She lifts up a prayer and she moves.

And when she moves with God, she often finds that God has been waiting for her to choose life. To choose possibilities and promises that she knows not of. She finds that God has already made arrangements for her happiness and her wholeness. She finds that God has hand-selected angels, both human and supernal, to assist her in her transitions to peace.

Whether right or wrong, my ministry was, and continues to be, a source of strength during a very unsure time. Not only was it flourishing and facilitating personal and vocational growth, but it also reminded me of the power that God has given me to curate my world. Yes, my preaching ministry was about the power of the spoken word, and its inherent ability to shape the atmosphere. But, in my case, my ministry also reminded me that my world—my personal world, my local world, our global world—is open to creative interpretation and constant re-creation.

I am mindful of the systems and the structures of this world that serve to stratify its inhabitants. Racism, patriarchy, white privilege, poverty, and so many more social sins throw the arc of the universe off, making its bend toward justice much more difficult to achieve. For years, I've been determined to assist this bend towards justice. But, over the years, I learned that I couldn't do this if I wasn't at my best, my fullest and my highest. I couldn't do this work and be burdened, especially when *some* burdens can be relinquished.

Curating a just world begins with curating a personal world that gives one a deep sense of authenticity. Because the truth is this: we are called to *everything*. We are called to ministry. We are called to parishes. We are called to vocation. We are called to people. We are called to relationships. And, if we are really honest, we can *feel* when we are living into these callings and when we are not.

About a year ago, I heard an art museum curator discuss her craft at a lecture at Trinity United Church of Christ, the congregation I am blessed to serve on the south side of Chicago. She talked about the essential nature of "inspiration" in the course of curating an exhibit. Information, history and understanding are important, but it's the inspiration that leads to the beauty. I remember her describing how an exhibit begins as a vision, a possibility. Its components come together collaboratively; the curator alone cannot accomplish the work. The art donors and collectors, the persons who install the exhibit, and certainly, the artists themselves, are just as crucial to the process. It takes time, investment, energy and effort to manifest a full exhibit. It demands the curator's complete mindfulness to placement, narrative, space, sound, and many other affects. By the time it comes into fruition, it has made a journey from nothing, and become something. As she described her idea of "inspiration," I could not help but equate her notions with my own ideas of how the Holy Spirit has moved in my life and ministry. This is how I approach my world these days: open to possibilities, following the inspiration of the Spirit, in deep need of community, and ever striving for greater balance and beauty, both within and without.

At best, the sermons in this volume articulate a theology of intentionality. Despite the variety in themes, aims, and intended audiences, they speak of a God who has great plans for the good of God's people, but a God who is looking for the people to take part in their liberation and to become active participants in the shaping of the world into the kingdom of God. Yes, it is God's vision for a just world, but God lights our hearts aflame, grants us a vision of that justice, and enables us to work, because we are called to bring this world into fruition. God gives us to one another, in just and loving relationships, to bring this world into being together. It's not enough to complain about our lives or our worlds. At some point, our tears and our prayers must give way to spirit-lead work.

This is what it means to curate a world: to see the sanctified vision that is ours to manifest; to hear the unique call that is ours to live out; and to respond in the affirmative. It means to come together; to do the work until the world is one that we can all inhabit in beauty, balance, love and justice. We can't stop believing that this world is the works, and that we are the ones who are responsible for its coming. We can no longer "wait for a new heaven and a new earth." We must work for them as if we *believe* that we will see glimpses of their coming in our lifetime.

These sermons reach back to 2012, and they chart my growth as a preacher and as a woman. In theme and in form, they attempt to achieve a theological aesthetic that reflects the audacity, beauty and justice of God. Therefore, they are not written in traditional form. Nevertheless, I pray that they will comfort and challenge you. I pray that they will inspire you and press you deeper into the call that is heavy upon your life. I pray that they make it impossible for you to ignore it or avoid it. Because as long as God is calling you, we are in need of whatever you have to offer. And, because as long as God is calling you, God will give you grace to live the calling out, as we curate this world together. It is my prayer that these sermons will meet you right where you are.

PART I

WOMAN WORDS

I could think of no better place to begin this collection than with a few sermons that were inspired by and prepared for women. As a young woman in ministry, I stand on the shoulders of women who were denied licensure and ordination, and of women who started their own churches and *denominations* in order to fulfill God's call. Black women in ministry have an illustrious history that emboldens me to preach in a manner that is unashamedly *womanish*.

In 2012, I started a work entitled *"shepreaches,"* a virtual destination for millennial Black women in ministry. Around this time, I began receiving frequent invitations to preach at women's events. I was developing a Womanist preaching voice, and I constantly challenged myself to raise issues that were pertinent to women, especially Black women. By doing this, I did my best to ensure that my entire self came with me to the pulpit and to ensure that women's stories and experiences came in from the margins of theological discourse and consideration in congregational settings.

Sexism and patriarchy are real in the Black church. However, I am thankful to be coming of age in a time where women have been my primary inspirations, models and muses in ministry. I have had women to look to for all of my professional and vocational aspirations. Women such as Rev. Dr. Claudette Anderson Copeland and Rev. Dr. Cynthia L. Hale have pastored me. These and others have shown me that it is possible to do this work, in this body. I have had Womanist theology to guide me in my theological thought and preaching. As a young woman who preaches, I am responsible for continuing in the way of clearing paths for my peers, and those who are coming behind us. If we continue the work that our predecessors started and if we do the work that will be unique to our generation, the holds of patriarchy and sexism will *have* to recede. I believe it.

In my ministry, I have made it my mission to speak powerfully, beautifully and truthfully to, about, and on behalf of women. I have made it my mission:

> To make room for our lived experiences in the pulpit.
> To shine a light on our spirits and to speak life over our dry bones.
> To curate spaces in which the multiplicity of our voices is heard loud and clear.

In so doing, it is my hope that I've disrupted the normalcy of patriarchy, and encouraged some sister in the process.

I'M IN A NEW PLACE

LUKE 1:26-45

Preached June 2012 at the United Church of Christ Black Women in Ministry Retreat, Bricks, NC.

Allow me a moment of personal privilege to talk about one thing that I simply LOVE about the Word of God. I love the women of the Bible:

> I love that there are women in the Bible.
> I love that women are depicted as people – humans – with complex stories and communities:
> Women with senses of humor and women with great faith
> Women who were rejected and women who ruled from Palm trees
> Women who said, "yes" and women who said "no"
> Women who bore many children and women who bore none
> Women with power and women on the margins
> Women who were friends with each other: Ruth and Naomi and women who had nobody
> Women with great names: Vashti and Esther
>   and women with no names: Jephthah's daughter, the Shulamite woman, and the woman with an issue of blood.

There are plenty of women in the Bible. And they represent a continuum. Yes, I like that for every season of my life, I can turn to the Word of God and find a woman whose story resembles my own, thereby allowing me entrance into the Word.

Now the only thing that I love more than the women of the Bible is the work that God does in the lives of the women of the Bible.

I love wombs that were written off as empty suddenly being filled with life. I love little drops of oil being stretched into countless jars of oil so babies could be fed. I love God showing up by rivers and creeks to disinherited women and saying, "I see you." I love healing shooting out into a woman's body from an article of clothing that was attached to the body of Christ. I love the dispensation of grace that occurred when a woman bowed down and anointed his feet with her hair, her tears, and her oil.

And I love when God does something in a woman's life, and suddenly she breaks out in song! Such was the case with Miriam in Exodus 15:20, "Then Miriam the prophet, Aaron's sister, took a tambourine in her hand, and all the women followed her, with tambourines and dancing." Miriam sang to them: "Sing to the Lord, for he is highly exalted. Both horse and driver he has hurled into the sea." And there are two women breaking out in song here in Luke 1. And what I see when women break out into song in the Scripture is that they have been shifted into a new place; moved from one place to another. Songs signify new places.

Here in Luke 1, we are allowed into the backstory of the birth of Jesus. The other Gospels seem to jump right into the birth of Jesus and the work of Jesus, but Luke takes a few steps back and tells us the backstory.

And it's unfortunate that this story is a backstory because this story has some amazing women in it. There are

> Faithful women,
> Godly women,
> Discerning, open, and willing women,
> Singing, worshipping, praising women, and
> Women who had conversations with God.

In this backstory, we get the idea that a whole lot went on before Jesus arrived on earth in the flesh, and this whole lot had a whole lot to do with some women.

I believe that there are a few women who know how it feels to be in the backstory. You're used to your quiet place in the background where nobody knows who you are or knows how much you pour out to make the way for a man to do what he does and do it well.

You know what it feels like to be behind the veil. To be

> Cranking the well so the water will flow,
> At the helm, turning the wheel so the ship can stay on course,
> And it always seems as if your part is the part skipped or minimized when the story is told.

Why? Because you are in the backstory.

But, there's a woman in the Bible who stands in community with those of us who are in the backstory—of our congregations, our families, our ministries, etc.—and who tells us that in the course of one divine conversation, God can move us out of the backstory and into the script, from the background to the foreground. With one word, God can move us into a new place.

Her name is Mary. You can say that in the course of 12 short verses, Mary was divinely shifted from an old place to a new place. Do you know what it feels like to be moved from one place to another place? Whether you wanted to be moved or not? God stepped into your familiar, got right behind you, and bumped you out of it. God reached God's mighty, powerful, providing, and protecting hand down, snatched you, and seemingly threw you out there with no power, no provision, and no protection? Or maybe God threw you into a place of greater power, greater provision, and greater protection? Maybe it seems as if God has approached you, real cool on the sly and said, "Sis, it's time to move. Let's go."

Well, what does it mean to get moved? Why does God move us, beyond the obvious reason that we can't stay in the same place forever? And what are the assurances that God has for us in a new place? Let's look to Luke.

1. The first thing we see is that forward movement is a mark of favor.

"Greetings," said Gabriel. "You who are highly favored!" These days favor has a popular reputation in the church. "Favor ain't fair," we say. We proclaim with great excitement that *favor* opens doors, increases net worth, and places us before mighty and powerful people.

I have a problem with a theology of favor that favors outward showings of God's grace and goodness most. I really have a problem with a favor theology that looks, sounds, and resembles prosperity theology. May I say that I've had some broke seasons where I had nothing and felt closer to God than ever, and learned to trust and depend on God as my source?

In this text, I see a very different theology of favor. Notice the order of things here: the greeting and affirmation of favor, *and then comes* the shift. It's almost as if God is priming Mary for the news that her entire world is about to change. You know that you have to hold on to your seat when God speaks words of affirmation because soon thereafter comes a word of instruction.

You have to enjoy those times of refreshing and refilling because just around the corner is someone that is going to come and drink it all up from you, and sometimes, God has to remind you that you are loved and favored and covered, right before your assurance in these areas comes under fire.

I rather like that the Word says that Mary was "very perplexed" at this greeting. Perhaps Mary knew God was up to something. Perhaps Mary knew God that wanted something *from* her and God wanted something for Mary.

I wonder if God thought:

So, you thought that you'd marry this nice fellow, Joseph, and live happily ever after? You had an ordinary plan for your life. I know that you're used to being in the backstory, and that you're cool with that. I know you're used to your privacy and your anonymity, but I'm about to elevate you and put you all way on blast.

I know you're young and you had a nice, run-of-the-mill plan for your life, but I am requiring more of you. Why? Because I am shifting you. I'm moving you into a new place. But before we move, I need you to know this: that you are favored and that I am with you!

I need you to know that
    I have gifted you.
    I have prepared you.
    I've brought you through all that you've come through and now.

You have gifts that nobody else has.
I can use you in ways that I can't use somebody else and I need you right now. So I'm about to move you. You're about to be moved out of the place you are in right now, and into a new place because I've been watching you, and I see something in you, something that I placed in you a long time ago—that will bring me glory. Now it's time to bring it to fruition.

Sound favor theology says that perhaps God will disrupt your comfort because God favors you. Perhaps God will publicize your pain because God favors you. Perhaps God will frustrate your plans because God favors you.

Perhaps the point of favor is not for you to accumulate more, but for you to come to see in yourself what God sees in you! Don't you remember? You said to yourself, "I never knew I had this kind of strength and resilience. I never knew that I had the skill of adjusting until God moved me."

But, as I've already said, favor can come with a cost. Favor comes with the cost of obedience. "Not my will, but Yours will be done." So, as much as you may resist your shift, as much as you fight it when God uproots you from what you know, you need to know that perhaps God is doing this because God FAVORS YOU. God sees what is in the new place, and God thinks that you deserve it. God sees how people will be saved, set free, and delivered through your ministry; and God wants to move you because God favors you!

Don't fight the favor. Don't resist the blessing. Go with the flow. Shift. Move, because you are favored! And, not only because you are favored, but more importantly, because God is with you! There was a second part of that greeting. "You are highly favored. THE LORD IS WITH YOU!"

Good news! Right before God gave her a new assignment, she received this word—this word of assurance. And, then came the news that she was being shifted.

2. She raised a question.

"How will this be since I am a virgin?" In other words, "God, there are some experiences that I have not had. Some experiences are usually *required* for this kind of thing to happen. How are you going to move me into a new place when I haven't had the *experience* that is required for me to do the thing that I have to do in the new place?"

And this was a good question because too often, we worry about qualifications. Do we have the background, the experience, and the aptitude to do well in the new place? It's exciting to be in a new place, but if we are really honest with ourselves, newness can be daunting not just because of the qualifications or lack thereof, but also because of the preparation question: *Am I really ready for this?*

We know that seminary never prepared us for a lot of what we have faced in ministry. Sure, you've completed your CPE, licensure, ordination, internships, fellowships, and research, but haven't you still found yourself caught out there at times?

But in a new place, when there is a disconnect between your experience and the realities of your new place, you're going to need more than this anyway. You will need something

More certain than your certification.
More real than your research.
More major than your Master of Divinity, or
More Divine than your doctorate.

3. You will need the Holy Spirit, the anointing of the Most High God.

"How will this be? The Holy Spirit will come upon you and the power of the Most High will overcome you." This new move wasn't about Mary and her power. It was about how open and available she was to being led by the Spirit of God.

There will be unusual new experiences—let the Spirit guide you.
New muck and mire—let the Spirit lift you
New darkness—let the Spirit light the way.
New heartbreak—let the Spirit soothe you.
New problems and predicaments—let the Spirit give you wisdom.
New people—let the Spirit show you who is for you and who is against you.

Let the Spirit
> Minister to you.
> Lead you.
> Shower you.
> Empower you.
> Equip you.
> Enable you.
> Release you.
> Renew you.
> Refill you.
> Walk with you.
> Talk with you.
> Move in you.
> Move through you.

Let the Spirit
> Save somebody through your life.
> Deliver somebody through your story.
> Sanctify somebody with your tears.
> Rescue somebody with your testimony.
> Birth something *out of you* that will save your community, your congregation, your neighborhood, this *world*, all to the Glory of God!

And, so not only is forward movement a marker of favor, but in your new place, you don't have to rely on yourself; God is with you.

Are you READY to receive the power of the Holy Ghost?
Are you READY to have the Spirit come upon you in new ways?
Are you READY to be overtaken by the power of the Most High?

Are you
> Ready for a new anointing? For a fresh rain and fresh fire?
> Ready to behold signs and wonders?
> Ready to see the lame walk, in the name of Jesus?
> Ready to see the sick healed, in the name of Jesus?
> Ready to see the oppressed be liberated, in the name of Jesus?

Well, if you're ready, come move into this new place. Come on! Come on over!

But, hold up! There's an additional important fact that you need to know. Just like it isn't about the level of your qualifications or preparation, it also isn't about your glory. When God moves you and fills you, you will have no choice but to give God glory and to give God praise because this was beyond you to begin with! So, we might as well, give God some prophetic praise for what God is getting ready to do in and through us in this season of shifting!

But, hold on to that celebration. Because after God affirmed Mary with favor and God's presence and told her that the Spirit would birth the Son of God through her, the text says that two other things happened.

Mary agreed to the task. Have you agreed? Are you sure you are on board? Is your heart fixed and your mind made up? Don't fool me or fool yourself. Have you *agreed*?

Then it says, "Then, the angel departed from her." I can imagine that Mary might have thought, "Seriously, God? You tell me something like this, and then just . . . bounce? You get my concession and my "yes," and then just leave?"

We've talked about loneliness. We've talked about isolation, and I've testified about my own deep displacement. I had a therapist. When I first started talking with her, I was in bad shape. This was almost a year and half after I had been shifted. Sad, lonely, confused, I was ready to give up and go somewhere else. For the first session or two, she just listened to me. And then, she came with the diagnosis. I had an Adjustment Disorder. She talked with me through it. And then she gave me a handout with some information on Adjustment Disorders. It read:

> "*Starting a new career, moving to a new city, being diagnosed with a major medical condition—any number of major life changes can result in stress. Many times people adjust to these changes within a few months; however, many others struggle to cope for some time. If you continue to feel down or anxious in response to a major life event, you may have an adjustment disorder. Adjustment disorder is a stress-related mental illness.*

People diagnosed with adjustment disorder feel anxious or depressed as a result of the stress caused by a major life change. Among those with an adjustment disorder, life may seem overwhelming and difficult to manage. Many times this results in serious consequences, and can significantly interfere with one's emotional, social, or occupational functioning."

It turns out that my new place had thrown me for a loop. I hadn't adjusted well to my new place at all. But to the outside, I'm sure it looked good. Newly married, moved to exciting Chicago, in a PhD program, called to Trinity United Church of Christ. But, the new place and all of its newness happened very fast and it shocked me. I had been snatched out of my old places. So, my question became very different. *What happens when your body is in the new place, but your mind, spirit, and soul have yet to get there?*

I told my therapist about it, and she gave me a diagnosis. Then she said, "You are experiencing this, Neichelle, but you also have a lot in your life to hold you up. You won't be in this place forever."

The new place won't be uncomfortable forever.

The new place won't be so shocking for much longer.

The new place won't be unfamiliar forever.

You will snap out of this and walk around in this new place with power, authority, and assurance. You will come out of this and into your new place.

And, of course, she was right!

You're favored. You've got the Spirit, And the new place won't be uncomfortable forever. But, let me close on this note. And it's in the text too. When she felt isolated and abandoned, Mary had to get moving so that she could go confidently into her new place. And not just move around anxiously or aimlessly. She went to Elizabeth. She went to someone who was on the same path, but who had been on the path a little longer than she had been.

She also went somewhere where she knew she could hear a word of encouragement. That's my final point; go get a word of encouragement. The text says that when she got to Elizabeth's house, that Elizabeth was filled with the Holy Spirit upon hearing Mary's greeting—upon encountering Mary in her new place.

Sometimes, you need to go and be with somebody who sees, who feels, and who discerns your gifts and who is excited about your elevation. Sometimes, you need to hear somebody say, "God is doing great things in your life!" You need to be around people who will suspend their jealousy and their judgment and their hateration to celebrate you in your new place. You need somebody's whose gifts and anointing jump around when you are in their vicinity.

In short, you will need girlfriends in your new place. I have seen a lot of women go it alone. Go through their lives by themselves. Go throught their struggles in isolation. Never reach out for support. Never ask for help. Never seek strength and shelter.

Don't you know that you can't do it all alone? Girl, you are in a new place and you will need someone to cheer you on in it, to pray for you in it, to cover you in it, and hold your arms up in it.

You will need someone to break out in song with you!

He has done great things for me, great things, great things! He has done great things for me!

I'm in a new place and
> *I will bless the Lord, oh my soul, and all that is within me—bless His holy name.*

I'm in a new place and
> *Spirit of the living God, fall fresh on me.*

I'm in a new place and
> *From the rising of the sun until the going down of the same, He's worthy. Jesus is worthy. He's worthy to be praised.*

Sing with me, my sisters! Don't let me sing by myself. Join in with me. I need you to help me.

Praise God, who favors us enough to shift us.

Who loves us enough to give us the Spirit,

Who calls us out of isolation and into song!

WHAT ABOUT YOUR BONES?

EZEKIEL 37:1-10 (NRSV)
PSALM 30:11 (NRSV)

Preached September 2015 at the Women in Ministry Conference, Atlanta, GA.

Several Sundays ago, I was in worship, in my favorite part of worship, the ritual of friendship, where we greet one another with a Trinity United Church of Christ "holy hug or holy handshake." I noticed that one of our deacons had a cast on her wrist. Concerned, I asked her, "Deacon, what happened to your wrist?"
"Rev. Neichelle, I broke it."
"How long will you be in the cast?"
"They weren't able to tell me. They said that they are going to have to see how it heals. Depending on how it heals for this first few weeks, they might have to put a new cast on, or let it continue to heal on its own."
Just this past Sunday, I saw her again, and I noticed that she was out of her cast. "You're cast is gone," I observed. "Your bone must be healed."
She replied, "Not all the way, Rev. Neichelle." Confused, I asked her why her doctors would let her leave the hospital with a bone that was still broken, but was not bound in a cast to promote its healing. "Well, they told me that my bone had a clean break,

and that it had realigned itself enough while it was in the cast, and that the remainder of the healing process could occur on its own."

Intrigued, I asked her, "Deacon, what exactly is a clean break?"

She went on to explain to me that a clean break occurs when a bone breaks quickly and when it breaks right down the middle. "When a bone breaks cleanly," she explained, "it is likely to heal more quickly, because the healing has more to do with the tissues of the bone coming back into alignment." I continued to probe with more questions, because this was getting good to my homiletical sensibilities, as it was quite amazing to me to hear how the body works when our bones break. I asked her another question: "So, they didn't have to break your bone when you got there?"

"No," she replied. "They would have had to break my bone if I had fractured my bone, in which case, my bone would've sat dormant, unable to heal itself because of the tension that the fracture puts on the bone. But, because my bone had a clean break, I didn't have to endure the pain of the doctors having to break it all the way." Interesting. What a distinction. This deacon was preaching to me and she didn't even know it. What she had just explained to me was a critical distinction between a clean bone break and a bone fracture. She'd basically said to me that while a clean break might be quicker and more painful initially, it is a much better condition to face than a bone fracture. And, while a clean break can also heal faster and heal itself after a certain point, a bone that is fractured must be *manually* broken all the way in order for the healing to even begin.

Sisters, as I look at the story of Ezekiel in the valley of the dry bones, I realize that we do not know if these bones in this valley were broken or fractured. We might assume that some aren't, but some certainly are. We don't know if they were clean breaks or if they were fractured. But, we do know that these bones represented a people in exile. A people displaced from the land promised to them, and given to them by the God who chose them for God's Self. They had been through a traumatic conquering at the hands of their Babylonian conquerors. The siege had been violent; they'd lost many of their own. They saw the holy city of Jerusalem and their temple to their God destroyed. They'd marched all the way into the homeland of the captors, and were greeted with a humiliating "welcome reception" as Nebuchadnezzar paraded them into Babylon as his prized colonized possession and the greatest of his royal accomplishments.

Soon after their arrival into the site of their chaos and their captivity, they were put to work. Their craftsmen and artisans were made to devote their skills to building up the empire and the economy of their captors. Their farmers tilled the land of their enemies, bolstering its sustainability and productivity. Some were imprisoned. Some were enslaved. All were in exile. You can read about their struggle in Jeremiah, 2 Kings and Ezra, but we hear of their despair in Psalm 137:

> "By the rivers of Babylon we sat and wept, when we remembered Zion. There on the poplars, we hung our harps. Our captors asked us for songs of joy, saying, "sing us one of those praise and worship songs you love." But, how can we sing the song of the Lord in a strange land?"

And through it all, there was a prophet named Ezekiel, who was called to pastor and to shepherd these displaced people in this strange land. We see that throughout this book, Ezekiel is a straight-no-chaser, passionate, and yes, quite misogynistic, prophet, who is clear with his people that they had *something* to do with their displacement. He proclaimed a just God, whose actions were always righteous, and even suggested that this exile was God's doing. And by the time we get to chapter 37, Ezekiel finds himself in a season of heightened envisioning.

This story is the third of four of his visionary reports, in which he sees—in the Spirit—his people being restored to their homeland and to their dignity. But this story has a particular problem.

My sisters, the problem in the text is that here we have a prophet who is charged with speaking life to dead bones, *but whose bones are also among the dead*. And not by virtue of his location in the spirit in this valley of dry bones, but literally within the context of the community which these bones represent. Ezekiel was also in exile, displaced from Judah in Babylon. He'd also witnessed the devastation of his people being conquered in their homeland and paraded into the site of their captivity. He was also at a loss, socially, culturally, economically, psychologically, and emotionally. But, he was still a priest. He still had responsibilities to the people of God, still had responsibilities to God.

Some sister in here knows that the call of God is not revoked just because *you're* going through something. The work of ministry and the devastation in the lives of God's people don't stop just because *you're* in a valley. No. The call of God goes on despite our struggles and our issues and, yes, even our pain. You have some days when all you want to do is crawl up into the bed, hide out, go off the radar, go underground, and the phone rings. The email pops up.

The people are in need because we're still getting shot in the streets.

> We're still suffering from mental health disorders.
> We're still losing our loved ones.
> We're still being profiled and targeted.
> We're still populating the prisons that make up the New Jim Crow.
>> Our women are still second-class citizens, vulnerable to all forms of violence.
>> Our men have yet to deconstruct and dismantle their internalized patriarchy.
> Our children are still afterthoughts.
> And you think that this work stops just because *you're* in a valley?

When the work still calls, what is it, woman of God, that keeps you going? What is it that prompts you up out your bed? What is it that interrupts your pity party and gets you back on your feet? Just like many of us, Ezekiel was isolated—and in pain. How could he not be? Just a few chapters prior, in chapter 24, Ezekiel hears a word from God that says, "I'm about to take away your wife, but you're not allowed to cry; you're not allowed to mourn; you can't adorn yourself as mourners; you must keep on working." He woke up the next morning, and lo and behold, his wife was dead. And here he is now—in a valley of dry bones. How could he not be in pain?

He has all this death, all the way around him. He is isolated in a valley, and yet he still has work to do. He still has visions to see, words of life and resurrection and new possibilities to utter over dead bones. He still has to talk to God about the people, on behalf of the people. So, before a word is ever spoken in this valley full of death, there is a very concerning scene here. An isolated and hurting prophet, on a tour of death, is viewing the consequence of the collective displacement of God's people. He is taking in the spiritual desiccation and festering bones of a people, *his people*, who are hungry for life and thirsty for resurrection.

While we are here to talk about being emotionally healthy preachers, I want to pose a fitting an urgent question: *what is to be said of bones of the prophet—the one charged with speaking the words of life and resurrection?* The preacher who has been set down in the valley, amidst death all around, not to mention the death within? I want to know who speaks to those bones? *Our bones?* What happens when our bones are cracking, dry, and easily broken? Where do we go? Who do we turn to for nourishment when there's no meat on *our* bones? As I look to this story for some answers, I'm drawn to a few things that I see here.

First, I am quite drawn and taken aback by the words of the first two verses of this story: *"The hand of the Lord was on me, and he brought me out by the Spirit of the Lord and set me in the middle of a valley; it was full of bones. He led me back and forth among them, and I saw a great many bones on the floor of the valley, bones that were very dry."* I am drawn to the way that God grabs this preacher to take him *into* a valley. Before a word of life or resurrection is spoken, God leads the prophet all around and among, back and forth, up and through, in and between these dry bones. God takes him on a tour of death, a survey of the land, and a brief time of diagnosis to assess the depravity of the valley.

I am drawn to the way that before God begins any work of resurrection, God wants the prophet to take the time to see the profound severity of the situation. God doesn't allow him to just come to the brink of the valley, take a look over the expanse of it, and then speak to it. God wants the man of God to be *steeped* in the death. God wants the prophet to *feel* it, feel it deeply, and feel it urgently. God doesn't want him to rush through the process of discerning the pain and counting the "very many" bones that were "very" dry. God wants the man to walk around in it. God wants him hear the sounds of the dry bones crackling together, perhaps cracking altogether under his feet.

God wants Ezekiel to hear the sound of the valley. There is no wailing, no moaning, and no crying out in exertion. Those sounds have given way to the unique sound of silence that is produced by death. God wants him to see that the birds of the air and the beasts of the wild had already had their feasts. He can see the teeth marks from those predators who left their hungry marks on the bones. He can also see that there was, therefore, no flesh; only dry bones and death.

I'm drawn to this because I believe that it suggests that there is no way for the prophet to move quickly to speaking resurrection if he wasn't *absolutely aware* of the extent of the peril in the valley. Perhaps he is witnessing to us that often, we want to move too quickly to healing, too quickly to restoration, too quickly to liberation and deliverance without taking the necessary time to survey the real condition of our own bones.

Have you ever thought that maybe your bones need to grieve? Need to mourn? Need to wail, need to shout, need to weep, need to unload some burdens—before they are restored? Ever thought that they've been suppressing some tension and that the time has come for them to release it? We don't walk around in our valleys, embracing their weightiness and their lowliness. We move too quickly through our valleys and try to climb out of them too soon, only to find that our bones are too weak to handle the climb. We want to move quickly to try to get out of the valleys, and we rarely stop to consider that maybe there is something *for* us in the valley, something that we can't get elsewhere. We avoid really looking at our bones, at our pains and frustrations, our fractured spirits and our dried-out dreams, because it hurts too badly to actually acknowledge that we're hurting.

How can you be an emotionally healthy preacher if you don't know how to sit with your pain long enough to figure out why it's there and what has it come to teach you? This text suggests that you can't raise up dry bones if you're not willing to look at them, listen to them, see where they are broken and where they are fractured. You can't speak to dry bones if you haven't taken notice of the fact that there are, as the text says, "very many" that are "very dry." We must understand that as much as you might like to get into the valley and get out, it's not always that expeditious. As much as you'd like to get there, speak over the bones and keep going to the next assignment without even looking back, *sometimes God won't even let you begin the work of speaking until you've done the work of listening to the bones.*

> What about your bones, sis?
> What are they saying to you?
> How are they doing?
> How are *you* doing, *really*?
> How's home?
> How's the family doing?
> How's ministry going, *for real*?
> Where are you with *you*?

Yes, you might have to walk around in the valley, my sister, but don't stay there too long. How are you going to get out of this valley?

The second thing to which I am drawn here is that, upon the completion of the survey, the prophet is speechless. Yes, sometimes, even *we* don't have words to say when we are faced with death in our lands and our communities—our lives. So, God asks the prophet a question, probing to check the status of his faith. I can see Ezekiel there, engaging God, in a way similar to the way that my therapist engages me. I can see them there in that valley, in a setup not completely unlike the setup at my therapist's office. I can see God standing across from Ezekiel, asking him this probing and personal question. I can see Ezekiel sitting across from God, trying to concoct the perfect response, while this big mess of a situation is right there in the middle of them. "Mortal, can these bones live again?"

Isn't it interesting how, despite knowing that we don't know always know the answer, we still play this game of politics with God? We quote every scripture in the Book. We put together the most thought out, theologically sound, logically tenacious, and even etymologically eloquent response, when the true truth is, "I don't know!"

> *I know that You're God and that You have all power, but I don't know about **these bones**.*
>
> *I know that You've delivered our ancestors before and brought them to their own wide-open space, but I don't know about **these bones**.*
>
> *I know that You've given us victory over and over again, but I don't know **these bones**.*

And if we're honest, we doubt the "resurrection-ability" of our bones because we know the *hell* they've been through. We know why they're crackling and broken. I know what these bones of *mine* have been through. I know their struggle. I know why they are so delicate, so sometimes I must admit, "God, I *don't know* if they can live again!" I appreciate the liberating queue that Ezekiel gives us here to just admit, "You know what God? Only You know." I believe it was this articulated honesty that moved God to show Ezekiel what he needed to do. He literally fed the prophet the words to say to initiate the work of resurrection. When we admit that we don't know, we move ourselves out of the way and give God the time, the space, the agency, and the permission to work—and look at what happens in the text. God works through the prophet to do this work.

Don't forget this: Ezekiel is seeing a vision of his people's condition in exile. Ezekiel is also in exile, so we might assume that his bones are also in the valley. His bones are also dry and decaying, and even he is proverbially dead. *The bones of the prophet also need a word.* This is what it means to live in pain in the public eye: to have a great need for a word, but be the one on whom the people rely for their word. If anyone needed a word in this story, it was the prophet.

While the people are dying, who out of us has time think about ourselves? While the people are languishing in their sinful and broken conditions, which of us has time to die or to mourn our losses? Who has time to really tend to *our stuff*, when we're so worried about who knows that we even have stuff? Who can tell that we got our own issues? You're so worried about your image and your pastoral presence and your reputation to even think about the state of your own bones. *What about your bones, sis?*

Ezekiel shows us powerful and good news. Sometimes, while we're languishing and while our bones are wasting away, we shouldn't wait to get to the conference to hear somebody else speak the word that we need to hear. Perhaps, if we get close enough to the mouth and the heart of God, God will give us the word that we need to speak to our own bones. Has it ever occurred to you that there's enough grace and power on your life for you to speak to the people *and to yourself?* Do you know that you are anointed enough, and that you carry so much authority in the Spirit, to speak to your own bones?

Wake up and realize, that sometimes we are called to the work of *prophetic multi-tasking: we must speak over the people and we must speak over ourselves—at the same time.*

In the words of my homiletics professor at Yale, Leonora Tubbs Tisdale, "you must preach the Word that you need to hear." As women in ministry, this might be what it means to save our own lives; to speak over our own bones and encourage ourselves. This might be what it looks like to self-care and work at the same time. Just like you can't wait for the summer to break after a long winter, sometimes you can't wait for someone to come along and minister to your bones. You know your bones. You know what they need. You know why they're in the condition they are in, and you must tend to them now before they break.

Can't you see Ezekiel's bones hearing the sound of Ezekiel's own voice speaking over them? Can't you imagine how excited his bones got when they heard the voice of their own? How would your bones feel if they heard YOU say to them:

My bones,
Hear the word of the Lord God:

Tendons and sinews are coming to you so that you can bend and flex again.
Flesh and skin are covering you so that you're no longer exposed.
New life is coming to you from the very mouth of God.

I ask you again, *what about your bones?*

Finally, I am drawn to the fact that the bones can't do anything without breath. The breath is what gives life to the bones. And, in the life of a bone, sometimes it gets weak, particularly in the lives of women. Our bones are unique in that they are more vulnerable and more susceptible to a condition known as osteoporosis, a state of gradual bone weakening over time.

The older your bones are,
The more they go through,
The more life they experience,
The more fragile they become.

Sometimes, you don't even know that your bones have become weak until one or more of your bones breaks, randomly and with very little pressure. They say that there are all kinds of things you can do to overcome this. You can take vitamins. You can get your calcium. The best way that researchers suggest to strengthen weak bones is to exercise them; move them; get them into something, some action, some movement. My research reveals that one of the best ways that a *woman* can strengthen her bones is by dancing.

Let me move my own bones, and allow me to share a story of my own bones, which have recently come through a valley known as divorce. There was one particular week in the course of this valley that completely blindsided me. Monday and Tuesday were fine. But, on Wednesday night, my atmosphere shifted when the spirit of mourning came over my heart as I was sitting in my girlfriend's house talking about ministry. My atmosphere was shifted on Wednesday night; and on Thursday, my lawyer called to say that our papers had finally been filed. I sat with that on Thursday, and on Friday, she called to tell me that the court date had been set. All of a sudden, the pain of my divorce came sweeping over me. After several months of buying my own home, flirting and entertaining the possibility of dating again, and generally enjoying being single and fabulous in Chicago, I began to feel what everyone said that I would feel. I began to feel what I had thought I was immune to. It's not that I was avoiding it; it's just that I was too happy to have a second chance with myself.

Despite knowing that I had to go through with this decision, and despite knowing that at the end of the day, I knew that it was either my marriage or my destiny. It would have been impossible to have both, despite knowing that the situation was a sure and certain slow, spiritual, emotional and mental death. The pain of the divorce suddenly and very sneakily broke in and interrupted the jubilation of my liberation. As the mourning and the grieving finally set in on Friday, I pressed my way through Saturday. Then, Sunday came. While some of us loathe Sundays because they can be so long, I still believe that when Sunday comes, God has *something* for me.

It was Sunday and I entered into the house of worship, which also happens to be the house of work. Since we're talking about living out private realities on public stages, I walked into the sanctuary with this grief as thick on my skin as my black robe was on my body. I sat in the pulpit, facing this massive congregation of people who came to receive something that I, as associate pastor, was partially responsible for imparting into their lives. But, as I sat there looking out, all I could think in my own spirit was *"it's me, it's me, it's me, O Lord, standing in the need . . ."*

This was one of those Sundays that I was glad I wasn't the senior pastor. Yet, I still had to be present, stand up, speak to the village, and charade like I was alright. Then our Sanctuary Choir began to minister this beautiful song. "You have no idea," the song said, "What God has done for me." Very briefly, I flashed back to all the other Sundays, sitting in that same place, suffocating from the being in the valley of the marriage. My bones began to move, and though I was in a different valley on that day, at least I wasn't in the same valley that I was in before.

I got out of my seat in the pulpit, walked out of the pulpit and found myself a corner. My bones and I needed a moment with our God. I let the song wash over me. I lifted my hands, and I let my tears fall. I let the Spirit take me around the valley in my own mind. And, as I did, I heard God say, loudly and *clearly*, "I will turn your mourning into dancing." I began to move there in that corner, just me, my bones, and my God.

Now, this isn't uncommon. Trinitarians will tell you that Rev. Neichelle takes off out of the pulpit to praise pretty regularly. But on this day, it was a special dance. It was a dance upon a promise that the Lord spoke directly to *my* spirit; to *my bones*. Not to me for the people, but to *me, and for me*. It was so tailored to my experience. It was so calming to my emotions. It was just the Word I needed to hear!

And so, I danced.

Moved by the Spirit, my bones resisted the weakness that was setting in from that week. Over the next several days, I spoke this Word over myself. I prophesied as I was commanded: "You have turned my mourning into dancing. You have taken off my sackcloth and clothed me with joy." I was amazed at how this shifted my perspective and my attitude. I began to realize that the worst of it was over. I rationalized to myself, "*Why be down when things could only be up from here?*"

Then the phone calls of encouragement came. Texts and e-mails arrived, reminding me that I am loved and not forgotten. The breath of God was blowing on me from every direction, all around me. I was hearing the sound of God's breath coming back into my bones, and I kept on dancing. Yes, even there in my valley.

As I close, it is important to note that what we see by the end of the scenario is that the bones—the once dry, once brittle bones are revived and the bodies have been resurrected. While I praise God for the new life, I also praise God that the people were *standing*. "A vast army," the text says. Notice that the text doesn't say that they got up and started trying to get out of the valley. No, it says that "they lived, and they stood on their feet," a vast multitude, standing—*in the valley*.

I'm sure you want me to move us out of the valley, but I can't do that right now. I can't because I don't want to undermine the significance of the valley.

Maybe God assigns us to valleys for a reason. Maybe God calls us into valley seasons for reasons beyond what we can appreciate, especially while we are in them. Valleys are low places. They can be dark, dismal and cold. Valleys are all about learning how to make it, despite undesirable and unbecoming circumstances and predatory elements.

Valleys are all about going into hiding, so that God can tend to you with some semblance of privacy.
Valleys are often enclosed by mountains and hills, so they are about learning how to navigate tight spaces.
Valleys are about humility, because there's nothing in them that screams comfort and convenience.
Valleys are about strategy, because even if you can't get out of them, you must be determined not to die in them.
Valleys are all about getting stronger for when you encounter mountains again, and things begin to shift and look up.
Valleys are for learning to wait on God, who promised that every valley shall be lifted up, and every mountain and hill will be made low. The uneven ground shall become level and the rough places shall be made plain (Isaiah 40:4)!

I thank God for my valleys. Valleys strengthen my bones. They teach me to dance in *despite*.

My sister, can you dance in your valley? Can your dry bones live again?

Finally, Ezekiel was not standing alone. I can imagine that Ezekiel's hope was renewed when he looked around in the valley, and saw that he wasn't alone. Isn't in empowering to know that you're not alone? I have to go, but I came today, to just remind you:

No matter the condition of your bones and no matter your private reality, *you are not alone.*

If you can strengthen your bones enough to stand, you will find that the air is lighter up here. And, when you look around, you are in a community of women who've been there, done that, and lived to tell about it.

Grab your sister by the hand, and testify, "I know that my dry bones will live again, because I can dance in my valley!"

IF JUSTICE WERE A WOMAN

MATTHEW 15:21-28 (NRSV)

Preached March 2015, Sojourner's Truth at St. John's UCC The Beloved Community, St. Louis, MO

Recently, I posted a status update on Facebook that said, "Please help me with a new sermon and complete this sentence. If justice were a woman, she would . . ." You should've seen the responses!

They ranged from the outraged:
"She would wipe out the land!"
"She would keep God in schools, educate our youth, and police our protectors!"

To the programmatic:
"She would protect the rights of her children."
"She would straighten out the imbalance in the scales of truth."

They ranged from the cynical:
"She wouldn't be a U.S. citizen."
"She wouldn't live in America because here she is exploited, disrespected, and not welcomed."

To the maternal and poetic:
"She would breastfeed the oppressed."

"She would give birth to restoration and peace."

"She would birth twins and name them Grace and Mercy."

From this, I learned a couple of things about how we imagine justice and the roles of women. For the past several weeks, we have all been watching with vexed spirits and broken hearts as a man charged with policing the people has gotten away with the murder of a precious son of God, Mike Brown Jr., and we have watched as his body laid on the ground for 4.5 hours. And we have watched as our own brothers and sisters have been tear gassed, shot with rubber bullets and treated like animals. And since here at St. Johns, and we are lifting up the work and the witness of the women today, I want us to consider the subject, *If Justice Were a Woman*.

If Justice were a woman, she wouldn't mind being an outside agitator.

This text suggests that if justice were a woman, she wouldn't mind being an outside agitator. The text says that Jesus was travelling to the vicinity of Tyre. And once he got there, he wanted to lay low. He went into a house and didn't really want to be bothered. By this point in his ministry, he'd gained a reputation that all he had to do was speak a word and miraculous things happened: boundary-breaking healings, system-subverting deliverances and spiritual right-settings and socio-political palpitations happened at the command of Jesus.

He was just one man. With the touch of his hand, with the words of his mouth—little by little, he was causing people to rethink what was possible for their lives. He was giving them hope for miracles again. He was revitalizing the possibility that they could live and flourish and be in harmony with God again.

So, *maybe* on this day, he would do this for her, this woman, this mother, this Syro-Phoenecian Gentile. She'd heard all about him. The rumors had made their way up to Tyre. And today, here he was, in the flesh. Here was her chance.

And it just so happened that she had a deep need. Have you ever had a deep need? A need for something deeper than water to drink, deeper than food to eat? A need for something deeper than sleep at night? I mean a *deep need*, a need so deep that it rocks your world. A need so deep that it feels like a gaping hole in your spirit? A need so deep that it keeps you up at night, wondering, *how am I going to*:

> *Pay my rent so I'm not sleeping on the street?*
> *Get through this grief over this huge loss?*
> *Feed my children so they're not hungry?*
> *How am I going to live through this terminal illness?*
> *How am I going to ensure that my child will come home tonight?*
> *How am I going to stand under the weight of this heartache and depression?*
> *How, God, are you going to work this out?*

I'm talking about deep needs. Needs so deep that you can feel them in the pit of your throat and in the deepest part of your gut. I'm talking about the kind of need that only God can meet. This is the kind of need that this woman came to Jesus with. "Lord, Son of David," she exclaims. "Have mercy on me. My daughter is demon-possessed and suffering terribly."

She tried everything else. She has a disturbed daughter whose battle with an oppressive spirit stole her joy and changed her beautiful personality. Her daughter had already been prescribed all the Adderall, all the Prozac, and all the Celexa that she could take. She sat with counselors. She saw the therapists, and no one could get to the root of the problem. Nothing worked.

She wasn't a bad child. She wasn't a delinquent student, so suspending her from school and threatening to expel her was not the way to address her issues. For far too long, everyone around her was treating her as if she was an isolated incident when the reality of the situation was that she wasn't alone in her disturbed condition. *All of her friends were also disturbed.*

The girls suffered from a lack of self-love.

They posted pictures of themselves on Instagram and Facebook, waiting with baited breath for the next like and affirming, celebratory comment.

They feared for their sexual safety. Boys ran through the girls like a hot knife in cold butter. Grown men didn't even care that they were underage. The girls felt like pieces of meat when they walked into a room or in public, and the sad reality is that some of the young ladies liked it. Some of them needed it to feel human, though it was totally wrong and perverted. A lack of male love and attention has made them all sick and hungry for *any* type of attention they could get.

The boys weren't safe in the streets either. They lived and moved through their neighborhoods and schools with moving targets on their heads. They were kids, who looked like grown men. They induced fear wherever they went, all the while fearing for their own lives. The stress of just living turned these once beautiful boys into ticking time bombs, set to go off at the slightest provocation.

In the text, the woman's daughter was disturbed with cause. She was disturbed because of the systems working against her personhood. She faced cultural and structural issues that were bigger than medicating and treating this one young girl.

This was a deeper need, and since Jesus was in the neighborhood, this woman decided that she'd take it to him. She would take herself to him. She would do her own agitating. The text says that she threw herself at his feet and begged him.

This suggests that if justice were a woman, she wouldn't be too proud to beg.

The situation of her child put her in an awkward position. Vulnerable. She couldn't hide how deeply she was in need. But, this was also awkward and difficult because she was different. The text interrupts the story to state, "She was Greek. She was from Syria Phoenecia." She was different.

And, difference is usually an interruption. It interrupts opportunity and access. Here, in the text and in our current society, difference can be a social, economic, political, and even a psychological challenge. It can impact where you can go without getting the side-eye or feeling unsafe. Instead of difference being a source of strength, it can often make us feel weak and marginalized.

Yes, there are some times, people and places where we can rightfully expect, "I may be treated differently because I'm different."

But, what do you do when discrimination and dehumanization shows up in the places you least expect it? Like in the church? Or within your family? At the doctor? What do you do when it feels like even God is in on it?! As if God is complicit in your oppression, when you *believe* that God can do something about it.

Yes, this woman's life testifies that while being an "outside agitator" can be uncomfortable and oppressive, it is often necessary when justice is on the line.

Finally, she would fight for what's right until she gets it.

"Stand in line and take your turn. The children get fed first. If there's any left over, the dogs get it." This was the response the woman received when she expressed her deep need to Jesus. Here, she shows us what we must do when discrimination and injustice show up, even in unexpected places.

After all she'd heard about him, she discovers that even Jesus had some issues, preferences, and biases that became public when he encountered this woman. It seemed as if Jesus had some racist impulses himself.

But she didn't hide from it. She didn't run from it. She exposed it. She spoke the truth about it. Even to Jesus.

"Jesus, I thought you came to seek and save all of the lost ones, but it really seems like some get found a lot faster than the rest of us." Now, there are some things that I could look over; some things that I could handle if they happen to directly to me because I understand the way of the world. But when the same thing happens to my child, it's on.

To be clear, I am not yet a mother, but I am an auntie. I will *go to bat* for my niece and nephews, even from afar. Our family faced one incident that was particularly traumatic. After almost four years in the St. Thomas More Catholic School in Atlanta, my nephew, who was nine at the time, began experiencing various forms of racial profiling by the school administration. Despite strong academic performance, he began to get into a lot of "trouble." The profiling that began with "time out" and removing him from social settings eventually escalated into repeated suspensions. We knew that something was amiss when he repeatedly claimed his innocence. His teachers began to fall silent, and only the administration seemed to have issues with him. One day, he got to school to find expulsion papers on his school desk. He was devastated. Our family was enraged and sought legal counsel; however, our options for taking action were limited because it was a private school. Upon enrolling him into a new school with a higher population of African-American students, we learned that many Black students transferred to this new school after having similar experiences at St. Thomas More Catholic School.

If there was ever *anything* that should light a holy fire within us it *ought to be* when our children are used as pawns used to uphold corrupt systems. It ought to be when our children become the victims of evil systems. It ought to be when our children's lives are at stake because some folk can't get their hatred in check. Then, **we ought not mind getting on our knees and negotiating for some justice, even if it means we've got to beg, holler, yell, or wail for it.**

If Justice were a woman, she'd put her every skill to work in negotiating for the lives of her children. If Justice were a woman, she would go where she wasn't invited and where she wasn't accepted, get on her knees and implore the Lord, "how long, O Lord?"

If Justice were a woman, she would be somebody's mother, somebody's grandmother, somebody's auntie, somebody's sister or "other" mother. She would work day and night to ensure that she left a better world for her babies than the world she inherited. She would get on her knees before Jesus, and pray until he changed his mind about some things. Then, Justice would get off of her knees, and on to her feet.

She would have the courage of Vashti, to say "no" to dehumanizing demands. She would have the foresight of Esther. When desperate times called for desperate measures, she went to king to negotiate for her people, saying, "If I perish, then I perish." She would have the fortitude of Deborah, to go into battle on behalf of her people. She would have the commitment of Jael, to finish the job of slaying systems of oppression. She would have the spirit of the wailing women, whom Jeremiah called for, to open the floodgates of heaven by opening the floodgates of their tears.

If Justice were a woman, she would wake us up every day and commit to doing the work, whatever her work was. She would pray for her children daily, call them each by name:

Grace, Mercy, Righteousness, Truth, and Hope.

Justice would open up the doors of her house to the stranger, get in the kitchen with Love and make a meal for the family of humanity, get it all on the table and invite us to eat it, right there in the presence of our enemy Injustice, our enemy Intolerance, and our enemy Hatred.

And, at the end of the feast, she would gather us in the living room, lay hands on each of us, anoint us in the name of the Lord, tell us the stories of God's goodness, and commission us to do our work in the world. Amen.

HANDING OUR BAGGAGE TO GOD: RESTORING THE DANCE OF OUR DAUGHTERS

JUDGES 11:1-10; 29-40 (NRSV)

Preached September 2015 at New Creation Christian Fellowship Women's Weekend, San Antonio, TX.

In 1971, genius choreographer and dancer, Alvin Ailey debuted a dance entitled, "*Cry*." The dance was a gift to his mother, and dedicated to Black women, "especially Black mothers," everywhere. In its debut, Judith Jamison, who would go on to become the Artistic Director of the Alvin Ailey American Dance Theater, performed the dance, and secured its place in the American artistic imagination. "*Cry*" is a 16-minute solo, composed of three parts wherein the dancer illustrates a trajectory that is common in the lives of many Black women. Over the three parts, we see a woman wrestle with bondage, and spin and leap her way into liberation. When asked about the experience, Jamison responded, "One of the hardest things to do is to finish it without looking exhausted."

Similarly, many of us go through such chapters in our lives. We go from bondage to liberation, and then from bondage to liberation all over again. And, we know that it is often very difficult to arise from a fight, to emerge from a season of fighting, without feeling exhausted and depleted, simply from the events themselves.

Not to mention the residual, the leftovers, the aftermath, the baggage that results from the battles.

As I've thought about these realities within the wider context of our lives, I've come up with just a few questions: How does one dance with all the baggage that she has accumulated and that she carries on a daily basis? How does one go through life with all of its contents, with all of its weight bearing down on our spirits, our bodies? And finally, I ask, how can we release the weight and restore the dance, and how can the sacrificed life of a little nameless daughter of antiquity speak to these questions?

So, before we begin speaking of this daughter in the text, let me see where the daughters are in the room. It doesn't matter how old or young you are. If you are a woman in here today, you are somebody's daughter.

You descend from your kinfolk, both known and unknown. You bear your kinfolk's name, some similar countenances, and perhaps even some inherited issues. You, who found yourself, young and female, born into a familial system with your lives coded with cultural gender norms. You found yourself beginning to piece together your identity by virtue of the relationships you shared with those you came to know as family.

Where are you, daughters?

I could be ruffling someone's feathers with this, because I know that being a daughter is often a very complex thing. I know that by bringing up the fact that we are all someone's daughters, that I am conjuring images and memories of your family:

> Your siblings, your blood siblings, and your sisters from other misters and brothers from other mothers.
> Your mama, your daddy—whether they were around or whether their roles were fulfilled by someone else, like your aunties, uncles, grandmothers and grandfathers.
> The ones who raised you and even the ones you raised. I know that I may even be reminding you of the way that you raised yourself and perhaps a few others. And now today, you only identify yourself as a daughter of God—*if that*.

I know that being a daughter can be complex. Even in the most ideal of daughter-to-family relationships, daughters are often charged with the all-too-dismaying task of figuring out what it means to be a "good daughter" inside of her family: One who is responsible and makes sound decisions, even at the cost of her *own* dreams and identity.

The "good daughter" is the one who is selfless and always thinks about her family first. She is the one who is diligent, following the plans that have been laid out before her or improvising creatively where there is no plan at all. You are someone's daughter. We are someone's daughters.

We are not alone in the room. Meet another one of us, another daughter. She can be found down deep in the annals of the Hebrew Scriptures and in the pew right next to you, alongside her family and her friends. Meet the girl, bright with a mind of deep thought and acute perception. The light of her dreams and hopes lights her aflame, and she is called apart for her potential and promise. The girl with the skill of warming hearts because joy like hers is rare, and hope, like the kind she possesses, is hard to come by.

She has a heart unfettered by distrust. She has a body that is always ready to break out in a dance and a spirit, enlivened by the very Spirit of God. She has a dance about her.

It seems as if music follows her. She is always seeking to celebrate someone, like a father home from battle. She is eager to love, eager to be loved. She is hungry for acceptance and thirsty for affirmation. She is always looking for joy.

She is looking for you to see her, to pay attention to her, to look beyond her budding breasts and her widening hips and her round derrière. She is more than a body, more than hair, and nails. She is a mind. She is a spirit. She is a soul. She is a child of God.

Yet, this girl is often looked over. She is often looked over in favor of the brothers and the sons. She is often misguided by images of flawless bodies and reckless love, until she's become lost on a search for *some kind of validation*.

She is often forced to carry more responsibility than her young back can hold up, and before she knows it, the young girl is fighting for her dreams, fighting for her divine identity, and fighting for her life. And, when in the fight for her life, she learns to do what it takes to survive. And, when surviving takes precedence over thriving—when it becomes more important that a young woman *merely makes it* and stops *deeply living*, she becomes intimately familiar with isolation, low self-esteem, and poor self-image. She loses her imagination, hope, self-sense, and maybe even her life. She loses her dance!

I believe that this girl's story has some answers to the questions we are asking. But, first, I need to get into the crevices of her background a little bit; because her background provides the context for her life.

Yes, she is caught in a matrix of her own issues, but her family history is such that it almost predisposes her to all of them. In other words, this girl was **born into baggage**. She almost has no say in some of the issues she navigates because she's inherited them. She's got bags for which she has no name, because she had nothing to do with their presence in her life. She did not pack these bags. This daughter was born into baggage.

Does anyone know what it means to be born into baggage? It means that you were thrust from the peace of your mother's womb into the complexities of this human experience. It means that you were born to imperfect people, imperfect families and communities, all of whom knew nothing about what to do with their issues, or how to release their own baggage.

This is just like the daughter in our text. Meet her father, Jephthah. Mighty judge. Valiant warrior. He is a man with his own bags that he never laid down. He has family issues. He was an "invalid" son because his mother was a "woman of the night." He was a rejected brother who got no share of his father's inheritance or his family's love. He has a destructive kind of piety.

You see, he was an unfathered *boy* – one who never had the influence of a father, never had anyone to hand the tradition down to him and teach him the ways of his people and his God. He never had someone to tell him that in the case of Abraham, God provided a ram in a bush—to keep him from sacrificing his son. No one told him that sending children through fire was not always pleasing to God. And, for a warrior whose concept of family was synonymous with rejection—one who never knew love, and who was never properly mothered *or* fathered—I find it difficult that he could conceive of a God who could be pleased without some act of physical or emotional violence.

Not only was she born into her father's baggage, but she was also born into the baggage of her larger context. She was born and raised in a place where her death was more favorable than bringing dishonor to her father. Her father was Jephthah, the Judge. He had just conquered the Ammonites and was finally about to be reunited with his family - on his terms. He was about to ascend to prominence and power since he had proven himself in battle. What would happen to him if *she* stood between him and his God, his world, and his image as a mighty warrior and a strong man at this critical time?

Furthermore, where was her mother? Where was *a* mother? Where was someone to tell her about the special way that God related to God's daughters? Where was a keeper of the wisdom of the women—someone to tell her that just a few judges ago, a woman reigned from a Palm tree, and another woman went to battle for her people and was victorious? Where was someone to tell her that women were not necessarily created to be in the background and to uphold a man's image just so he can feel "macho" or project a "macho" image.

And so, not only was she born into the baggage of her family and the baggage of her context, but she was also born into the baggage of crucial absences. The daughter had bags before she was born. Bags were imposed on her. Bags are all around her. Many of her problems were related to her status as a daughter.

I wish I had the time to get into the story, the intelligence to understand it and the answers as to *why* God let this happen to this girl. The truth is that I know that a lot of us in here—sons and daughters—have lived with that very question. *God, why did you let this happen to me?* Whatever *this* is. We've wondered why God didn't intervene for us the way God did for somebody else. *It* just wasn't, or *isn't*, fair. *I didn't choose these bags!*

As this text and our lives boldly profess, God's ways are not always fair in our minds. God doesn't deal with us in terms of fairness. But what God does do is give us the strength to keep going on and the power to drop our bags—to keep dancing—until those answers come. Although her dance and her life were taken this daughter's life gives us some suggestions for restoring our daughter-dances in the final verses of chapter 11.

She came out dancing.

When I was growing up, I remember that around every major holiday, our grade school art projects would consist of handmade greeting cards and gifts to give to our parents. Mother's and Father's Day, Christmas, Thanksgiving, Easter. It seemed as if very early on, our teachers wanted to show us that there is an intrinsic value to what we could create as children. We didn't have any money, but there was something that we could give to express our creativity and our love. Throughout my life, this is something that I've struggled to maintain because I've become inundated in what I now know to call capitalism. Even with the memories of how those greeting cards would adorn Mom and Dad's offices and refrigerators, I still struggle to put in the time and the energy and the thought and intentionality into *creating* something *authentic* instead of going out and spending my money on mass-produced gifts.

This is why I love that this daughter chose to bless her father with a dance. It was an act of expression and joy; it was a display of her unfettered love and excitement that Dad was home, victorious in battle. She didn't know just how much was riding on this dance, but she came out of the house dancing. Did she receive the word that the Lord had given her father victory over his enemies? Or, was she just so excited to hear her father returning home, to learn that the Lord had spared his life in battle, to see him with her own two eyes? I can imagine her young feet prancing as her hands held the tambourine, dancing just because her dad was coming home. Dancing because that's what she did. If she were a runner, maybe she would have run to see him. If she were more of an analytic than an artist, perhaps she would have walked to meet him. But, in her creative genius and her artistic impulses, she came playing the tambourine and dancing to meet her father.

And in the course of her dance, she is met by her wailing father and the news that she has received a death sentence. Can you imagine this girl, dancing to the beat of her own drum, when all of a sudden, her beat and her dance are stalled, and her life is stolen? How many times have the creativity and artistry, the eccentricity and the expression of our daughters been squelched because their families didn't understand them or accept them? How many dreams have died because a child was told to forsake the dream and chase the check? How many gifts and talents have been thrown away because no one clapped for her or cheered for her?

How many beautiful heads have hung down low because they were never told that they were beautiful? How many of our daughters' voices have been silenced because they were ignored for too long or told to quiet down? How many of her possibilities have been foreclosed because she wasn't affirmed, and wasn't strong enough to affirm herself? How many of our daughters have lost their dances? How many of our daughters' dances have been replaced with weeping and roaming, or even dying?

In a culture that has convinced our youth that they live with their lives on the line, it seems hopeless that the dance can ever be recovered. She came out dancing, and her dance suggests that restoration of the dance begins with a re-membering of that which was authentically her. This daughter prompts us to ask ourselves, *what gives me life, and gives life to my bones? What makes me want to dance? What comes so naturally to me that I couldn't shut it up or stop it, even if I tried?* As Howard Thurman said, "Don't ask what the world needs. Rather ask, 'What makes you come alive?' Then go and do it! Because what the world needs, is people who have come alive."[1]

She received and conceded to her father's fatal decision, but not without some negotiation.

Although she was a girl in a patriarchal context, she spoke up for herself. "You will have to do what you've promised, but not before I get two months to mourn." How many of us have resigned ourselves to carry this weight, this baggage without negotiating how much we can really handle? How many of us do this without raising questions and gaining clarity? How many of us of have exercised some boldness and asked for what we need? One of the most tragic consequences of baggage is that it convinces us that we are not worthy of better. We get used to carrying it. We get used to its weight and its pressure. So much so, that it becomes a part of who we are. We don't stop and ask ANYONE for what we need and what we deserve!

When was the last time you asked somebody for *help* because you simply needed some help? Or called a licensed therapist because you needed to clear your head before a strenuous condition set in? Or asked the boss for a raise because you *needed* more money to support you and your babies? Or asked your partner for a greater degree of intimacy because you needed it? Or asked your best girlfriend to get on a plane or get in her car or whatever, because you needed some girlfriend time to bring you back to center?

Do you know how to ask for something life giving? For something that is good for you? Do you know how to ask for what you need? My sister, do you know how speak up for yourself? Better yet—do you know how to *show up* for yourself? Do you know how to advocate for yourself? Do you know how to do something to help yourself; to *obnoxiously impose* yourself in order to ensure your own sanity, like the woman at Bethany, and the woman with the flowing blood, who *spoke up for themselves?*

Or, have you resigned yourself to living with dead weight? Have you resigned yourself to silence and to this heavy lot in life? Do you know how to stand on the picket line with your sign, on strike until your own needs are met? Or is it that you do not believe that your needs are important enough? Do you not value your own humanity, or know the sound of your own voice?

Let me remind you that you, woman of faith, daughter of God, come from a line of women who knew what it meant to negotiate with God. You have been invited to negotiate! You've been invited to represent yourself, to speak up for yourself and to act on your own behalf. *Ask and it's yours; seek, and you'll find; knock, and the door will be opened to you.* If you want to restore your dance, you will need to speak up for yourself. Ask for what you need!

Finally, she went to the hills.

She went into a remote and hidden place, to mourn what would never be. She didn't go to mourn her death. She went to mourn what she would never experience. What happened up there? The text says that she wept with her friends.

Grief is the ache that results from some detrimental loss—in the privacy of our hearts. It is the process by which our souls go through the valleys of life. Mourning, on the other hand, is what happens when that ache is made public. It is the wail, the shout, and the releasing of the tears. It is the disclosure and the representation of our pain. What made it public is that she didn't go up all by herself. She went up there with her girlfriends. She didn't go through this alone. She took some of her sisters with her.

Now—there is the friend who will kick it with you when the kickin' is easy; yet, at the sign of difficulty, she's nowhere to be found. Then, there is a girlfriend who will be *with* you when things get thick and when they get thin. These are the girlfriends who can *handle your hills*. I believe that there are some of us here that would say that a girlfriend—a God-sent girlfriend—can mean the difference between life and death, surviving and thriving, and giving up and getting up and going on.

So, this daughter takes to the hills to let it be known that she was hurting. However, rather than living on with that hurt—that baggage—and taking it with her to her grave, the hills became a site of release and sharing. There is good news here! Perhaps you've lost your dance because you were dancing solo. The solo just seemed easier. With a solo, you don't have to wait on somebody else to rehearse. But somebody knows that a solo is more difficult. You have to carry the performance all by yourself.

Somebody knows that sometimes, a duet or a company can make the load a little lighter. It may take a little more work. But, the restoration of your dance must often involve other people, perhaps even some girlfriends. Ecclesiastes 4:13 says that, "One can be overpowered, but two can defend themselves. And three is even better because a cord of three strands is not easily broken." Girl, you've got to be able to admit when you can't get your dance back by yourself. You need some girlfriends.

You need someone who can bear witness to the power of God, who reminds you of the God you serve and the promises God has made to keep you. A *girlfriend* who can remind you, "*You've been through this before. God has fixed this before.*" And one who will bear witness to what she sees in you, and will tell you, "*You can do this! You can beat this. You can win this!*"

I'm so glad that we don't have to look to the hills to mourn anymore. We can look to the hills from which cometh **our** help. Our help comes from the Lord. David said, "I will lift up mine eyes to the hills from which cometh my Help. My help cometh from the Lord, The Lord who made Heaven and earth. God will not suffer my foot to be moved"[2] because God is *my help*!

When I hear the words of David, I begin to hear the voice of Jesus saying—

> "And I will ask the Father, and the Father will send you a HELPER"—
> An Advocate when you don't have one,
> A friend when you don't have one, and
> A voice when you don't have one.

God will send you the Spirit of Truth, Who will cause you to remember and re-member the dance that God gave you. God will send you the Spirit who will give you boldness to speak up and show up for yourself. God will send you the Spirit who will draw you to the hills to mourn, to release, and to share.

The good news is this: there are young women who may have lost their dance at one point, but who lived on to get it back, because of the Spirit of God. There are women who may have lost the beat and the rhythm of the music, but hung in there to hear it again because of the Spirit. And, this young girl lives on in the woman who decides that she is ready to resume her *dance*. She says, "Dance, dance, dance; show off all of your moves!" She can do it—we can do it—because of the Spirit who beckons us to be restored; the Spirit who restores us all so we can dance! Women, go ahead and dance, dance, dance!

Notes

1. See Gil Bailie's *Violence Unveiled*, p. xv, where he attributes the quotation to a conversation he had with Thurman.

2. Psalm 121 (paraphrased)

I HAVE A QUESTION

JOHN 11:1-5; 20-25

Preached on Good Friday 2014 at the inaugural shepreaches Good Friday worship service, "Seven Songs and Sermons in Honor of the Savior," Chicago, IL.

"When the summer came you were not around
Now the summer's gone and love cannot be found
Where were you when I needed you-last winter, my love?

When the winter came you went further south
Parting from love's nest, leaving me in doubt
Where are you when I need you, like right now?

Our love is at an end
But you say now you have changed
But tomorrow will reflect love's past

When the winter came you were not around
Through the bitter winds love could not be found;
Where were you when I needed you, last winter, my love?

Our love is at an end
But you say now you have changed,
But tomorrow will reflect love's past oh

Spring will fill the air and you will come around,
With your summer love that will let me down,
Where were you when I needed you, last winter, my love?"[1]

In the words of my home pastor, Claudette Copeland, "every relationship needs questions." No relationship can thrive without questions.

> Questions: linguistic expressions used to make a request for information.
>
> Questions: tools by which we mend the breaches of our understanding; means for bringing calm to our confusion.
>
> Questions: the light-switches by which we attempt to illuminate our darkness. Bridges between our assumptions, our presumptions, and our observations—and the real truths of the matters of our lives.
>
> Questions: a way into deeper conversation, deeper understanding, and deeper clarity.

It is often when we are confused, upset, frustrated, or simply when we are trying to get on the same page as someone else that we must ask questions.

Young people, you know something about the questions of your parents: Where are you going? Who will be there? Will there be adults there? What time are you going to be home?

To the married people in the room, you know something about the questions of your spouses: Where are you going? Who will be there? Will there be adults there? What time are you going to be home?

Through questions, we can dissipate our curiosities and clarify our confusion. Through questioning, we can probe when we are suspicious. Some relationships operate under the *modus operandi* of "don't ask, don't tell." Nine times of out ten, if you were to ask the parties of such relationships, they may tell you that they suffer from a stifled sense of security, a jilted sense of love, and a constant fear of the unknown. Because where there are no questions, there can be no light, no faith, no development of trust, no cultivation of confidence, and no accountability.

I'm just familiar enough with the ways of people to believe that no matter who you are or where you are in life, you, too, have some questions.

You may have some questions of yourself, such as:
When am I going to get it together?
Why do I keep doing 'x, y, z?'
What was I thinking?

Or, maybe you have questions of someone else:
Do you really love or care for me?
Why do you keep on doing 'x, y, z?'
What were you thinking?

Maybe you have questions for the world:
Why do some women sell out to patriarchy, resorting to making sex tapes and objectifying themselves for fifteen minutes of fame?
Why is racism still so operative, and why is the plantation model of "leadership" so obviously replicated in the world (see the NBA, NFL, and the NCAA)?

Or, maybe you have questions for God:
Are You going to come through this time?
Why are You taking so long?
Do You really forgive me for what I did?

Yes, as people in relationship with God, sometimes we get confused when it seems that God's actions are contrary to what we know, believe, or have previously experienced of God. When this is the case, we have to ask God some questions.

This is why Mary called Jesus to account when she told him, "If you had been here, my brother would not have died." In other words, "where were you when I needed you?" She asked this because of the relationship she and her family had with Jesus. We know that they had a tight relationship with Jesus. The home of Mary, Martha, and Lazarus was in a town called Bethany, a place where sickly outcasts and rejected ones lived. It was a humble place, probably much like Jesus' hometown of Nazareth. Jesus loved these three siblings, and their home was where he went to get a little rest and rejuvenation amidst his hectic ministry schedule. It would not be too far-fetched to say that all the love that Jesus could stand was in this house.

Since Jesus commanded that we must love God with all of our heart, soul, mind and strength, one sees that all of this was there in the house of Mary, Martha, and Lazarus. At their home, he could get delicious food for his stomach and stimulating conversation for his mind. From Martha, he could receive worship and adoration that warmed and moved his heart. From Mary, he could get the support of a big sister, and from Lazarus he could get the strength gained from brotherly love. So, of course, Jesus loved Mary, Martha, and Lazarus.

And, here is the trouble in the text: Mary, Martha, and Lazarus, find themselves in a bind that Jesus could easily fix. Rather than fixing it, Jesus knowingly, intentionally, and purposely withdraws his presence from them. This goes beyond *"I have other things to do."* Beyond, *"I'm busy and I just can't make it to you right now."* Or, *"something critically important came up and I couldn't get there."*

No, this withdrawal was purposeful. It was more along the lines of, *"I know that you're in a bind. I know that you're in a situation that seems to be getting worse and worse by the day. And while I could choose to come to comfort you and console you, to turn the situation around before you give up hope, I'm not. I'm choosing not to immediately run to your rescue. I'm choosing not to immediately come and stand by your side."*

Yes, there's trouble in the text because even if Jesus didn't fix the situation, Jesus could have at least been there to make it more bearable. Jesus could have been there to keep watch with Mary and Martha. Jesus could have been there, just to show that he loved them. But, instead, Jesus "stayed two days longer in the place where he was."

And his was a costly absence.

> The absence of HIS presence allowed for the severity of the illness to increase.
>
> The absence of HIS presence allowed for the setting in of hopelessness.

The absence of HIS presence meant that the days were getting longer and the nights more unbearable.

The longer Jesus was not there, the worse the sickness got.
The longer Jesus was not there, the louder the voice of doubt and fear became.
The longer Jesus was not there, the greater the heartbreak and disappointment.

Anybody know about the absence of Jesus? Anybody ever had to ask, *My God, my God, why have you forsaken me?*

Yes, the absence of Jesus is so devastating, so disorienting, so completely problematic that it can feel like a slow death.

Mary and Martha knew it. When someone's actions do not reflect your relationship with them, there is often the immediate need to raise one's voice. And I understand that many of us, as women, sometimes struggle to speak up. Yes, even *us*, as "loud, proud, headstrong and assertive" Black women struggle to speak up for ourselves. Sometimes, we struggle to think that it would be "worth it" to speak up, or we wonder if we'll even be heard and acknowledged. Sometimes, when we speak, we hear our voices trembling and we hear them crackling. Sometimes, when we speak, we feel our palms sweating and we our pulse escalating. But, sometimes, we don't have any other option, *but to say something.*

Sister, you know how it is when our silence would certainly be more costly than speaking up. Silence can kill the soul. Silence can break the spirit. Silence can steal your dignity. Silence will signify that you don't care. Zora Neale Hurston once said that, "if you are silent about your pain, they will kill you and say that you enjoyed it." Sister,
when you are confused,
when you are hurting,
when you have been mistreated, and when
people who *say* they love you and treat you otherwise,
you *cannot* remain silent.

You have to find your voice.
You have to *raise* your voice.

You have to open up your mouth.
You have to *say something*.

And sometimes, like Mary, you need to ask questions. Jesus' absence didn't reflect the nature of their relationship, so Mary *asked* him about it. She *asked* about *his absence*.
"Where were you when I needed you?!"

She may have been nervous, but she **asked anyway**.
She may have been afraid of his response, **but she asked anyway**.
She may have thought that it was wrong to question the Son of God, but **she asked anyway**.

I like that she asked because it shows that asking doesn't mean that you don't believe. It doesn't signify the absence of faith. It signifies a relationship that has reached the point of a question, that's all.

If you allow me a moment of personal transparency, I must admit that sometimes I struggle with the voice in my head that tells me "don't question God." The voice says, "Even if you are confused, don't question God." I have to fight with that voice because after all, it's my belief that God is not the author of confusion. I have to fight that voice because it is my belief that God does not lie. Therefore, it should be my custom to ask questions to discern the truth for my life.

After all, since God is the Wonderful Counselor, God just might be able to handle it when I go and ask, "Lord, why did that child die at the hands of a child who looks like them? Why did that father walk out on his children and never look back? Why do our people continue to be slain in the streets by the police? Lord, why?"

And because it is my belief that God will not forsake me or won't turn God's face from me for asking, sometimes, I have to ask God for myself:

Where were you when I needed you?
Why didn't you stop me from making that bad decision?

Why do I have to keep asking you for the same thing over and over again?
Why didn't my family member rebound from that sickness?

But if I could be honest with you again, I'd rather go to God with some hard, sticky, and shameful questions than suffer in silence. Is there anybody in here that can relate? Do you have some questions for God? The text shows that Jesus can handle questions. And, that we don't have to suffer in silence with the fear that we shouldn't ask God any questions.

Not only was Jesus open to her asking the question, he was also available to give her the answer *because of the nature of their relationship*. Because of the relationship we have with God, full of grace, mercy, and love, we can come to God with questions.

Not only do I love that she asks, I love what Jesus does: he answers! He says, "I am the resurrection and the life." You see, when questions arise in relationships, it's one thing to get a direct response. If you give it some time and pay close attention, you will also *see* the answer.

Does he or she love me?
Should I make this huge move?
Is this the right time, right job, rights situation for me?

Sometimes, our answers don't come immediately. They come over time, in stages and phases. Sometimes our answers don't come in the form of spoken responses, but in showings, signs, actions, and maybe even miracles and wonders.

He said, "I am the resurrection and the life" and then he **shows** her. He **shows** her what these metaphors can amount to in her life.

He shows her that by "I am the resurrection and the life," what he really meant was that death couldn't stand in his presence. He meant that death was antithetical to who he was, and that all things could live again in his name and by his power.

And so, maybe today, for those of us who are living with some questions for God, we ought to raise our voices, and offer up to God a new prayer!

Lord, don't just give me an answer, show me,
> Show me healing from cancer and HIV/AIDS in our communities;
> Show me family members who forgive each other;
> Show me deliverance from our addictions;
> Show me by fixing our self-hatred;
> Show me relationships rescued from domestic and sexualized violence;
> Show me a redeemed justice system;
> Show me something I've never seen before;
> Do something that only You can do;
> Show me in a way that I can't doubt it or dispute it! Show me your glory!

And on this Good Friday, I'm grateful that Jesus is committed to practicing what he preaches and to *showing* what he says, not only in Mary's life, but also in *our* lives. Since it's Good Friday, where can we go but to the Cross? At the cross, he showed us. At the cross, He went beyond his words when they hung him high. He went beyond his words when they stretched him wide. He went beyond his words when they nailed his hands and pierced his side.

And because of what Jesus *did*, there is no question about my status and your status. We are saved! There is no question about our identity. We are the sons and daughters of God. There is no question about whether we are loved. For there *is* "no greater love."

At the cross, he answered our most serious questions. At the cross, he answered old questions, and he gave us a new question: "Lord, why do you love us so?" To this, we may never know the full answer, but we should just rejoice and be glad that He does.

Note

1. Stevie Wonder. *Superwoman: Where Were you When I Needed You Last Summer?* From the CD Music of My Mind. Uptown Universal, 1972.

PART II

JUST WORDS

These sermons were inspired by the struggle of my people. I've been a student of Black History for many years, and over the past few recent years, I have seen this history repeat itself in ways that I never imagined I would see in my lifetime. Growing up, my friends and I would *hypothetically* discuss, "if you were alive back in the Civil Rights Movement, would you be on the Martin side or the Malcolm side? Would you be a Panther?" We never thought that we would have to decide how we would show up in a movement of our own.

I also would have never thought that I would be a woman in ministry, and that I would be a preacher when during this movement. During this time, my theological convictions haven't allowed me to keep silence. Preaching *justice* has become my homiletical and vocational non-option. Furthermore, I have been pressed by *Black Lives Matter* to refine my own notions of what ministry is, and what is requires of me as a servant of God. I, like many, have been inspired to learn from activists, past and present, whose efforts have made all the difference for the condition of our people. I have thought very carefully about the intersection between the words I preach and my witness beyond the walls of the church. I, too, have been involved in direct actions, under the leadership of young activists. I, too, have been involved in town hall meetings and teach-ins, so I could learn and so that my ministry will be ignited by a more keen awareness of the issues that are killing our communities. It is my prayer that the Kindom of God has come closer for our collective efforts.

I dedicate these sermons to the young activists who have carried this movement, particularly in Chicago, where our streets are drenched in the blood of Black men and women.

Black Youth Project 100 Chicago
Assata's Daughters
Fearless Leaders of the Youth
We Charge Genocide
Black Lives Matter Chicago
Budget or Else
Fight for 15

And all of you.
Thank you for what you do.

JESUS IS STILL AT THE TABLE

MATTHEW 26: 6-13 (NRSV)

Preached April 2012, Trinity UCC, Chicago, IL

Two weekends ago, I saw a great movie entitled *The Visitor*. During the course of this film, I was drawn into the lives of the main characters through the intricate intertwining of different genres of music. Against a backdrop of a fusion of classical, Caribbean, Afrobeat and African music, I was introduced into the lives of Walter Vale, a White upper-class college economics professor whose recently deceased wife was a classical musician, and to whom he was desperately trying to hold on to her by learning how to play the piano. We were introduced to Zainab, a beautiful Senegalese woman, an artist and jewelry designer who was in a relationship with Tarek, an equally beautiful Syrian man, whose passion for playing the djembe was matched only by his passion for living. Over the course of the film, these three lives became intertwined. So much so that by the end of the film, after learning that Tarek and Zainab were living "illegally" in America in Walter's New York apartment, and witnessing Walter's transformation for having met them, I wasn't quite sure who *the visitor* was, and had to be content with the fact that we are all visitors somewhere at some point in time.

Although we would all like to belong in all places at all times, we must all deal with the feelings of being out of place, outcast, or even alien in some places, around some crowds, and during some seasons. You know the feeling of being in such a place and looking for one friendly face, one warm smile, or one indication that you're welcome and that your visit will be a good one. And we know the feeling of that indication never coming. It is a cold and isolating feeling when you know that you are not welcome. Consequentially, we vow never to return to that place, to that crowd, to that season ever again.

In the text, we see that this is a common human experience. We are always living within some preconceived boundary, in the same way that we are always creating them. It is true that we won't always "belong," that sometimes we're not right at home. Where do we look for a welcome? Who can we turn to? What do we do in unwelcoming spaces? Let's see if this text can't help us unearth some answers.

1. And the text says, Jesus was in Bethany in the home of a man known as Simon the Leper . . . ."

Bethany is a small village near the Mount of Olives, just east of Jerusalem. It was home to Mary, the romantic worshipper, who loved her some Jesus, who couldn't pay attention to anything but Jesus in his presence, and whose world stopped whenever Jesus was around.

Home to Martha, the alleged busybody, whose reputation for working in Jesus' presence instead of worshipping there fails to pay honor to her intention to simply make a space, or perhaps set a table that was appropriate for Jesus' comfort.

Home to Lazarus, the once-sick, then-healed man. The once-dead, then-resurrected man. The man who was saved by his sisters' faith in Jesus, Jesus' fearlessness of festering flesh and his power to raise the dead out of pure compassion.

Bethany is a place of respite for the poor and healing for the sick. It is a place that Jesus frequented throughout the Gospels. This casts Bethany in a light of utter paradox and exciting possibilities. If it was a place inhabited and frequented by the poor and the sick, and *if* it was a place frequented by the nomad Jesus, it must have also been a place in which the possibility for healing and for provision were frequently at hand, just because Jesus was present.

Bethany was a site of some *unusual* activity. Of course, we know that it was the site of Lazarus' stunning resurrection, the breaking forth of life from death at the words of Jesus, "Lazarus, come forth!" and a subsequent command to all the onlookers, "Unbind him, and let him go."

And here, in this scene in Bethany, there is a meal going on in the home of Simon the Leper. It makes sense that Simon would live here. As a leper, he was more than likely banished to the outskirts of the city. And now, as one who had been healed, he chose to remain there. However, this meal was an exclusive, invitation-only meal. Simon has a point to make to those of us who've been delivered from *something and* want to act like we've always been delivered. These are those who want to walk away from their deliverance and act brand new, quickly forgetting who we were before Jesus came into the picture.

But, I digress. Here we are in Bethany in Simon's home, at his table. An everyday occurrence, but much like today, there were some interesting politics over who was allowed to eat at certain tables. In fact, eating was the afterthought at ancient tables. According to liturgical scholar, Nathan Mitchell, "A table's prime function was to establish social ranking and hierarchy, based on what one ate, how one ate and with whom one ate. A meal was about social identification, status, and power."[1]

But something radically shifted when Jesus was **at the table**. When Jesus was **at the table**, these politics had to shift. Jesus had a growing reputation as a man with no honor, no shame. He obtained this reputation for his inclusion of marginalized people in his ministry and at his **table**. Jesus practiced a different table politic,

A *come as you are* politic
A *come unto me* politic
A *whosoever will* politic

When Jesus was **at the table**, Jesus spoke with tax collectors, moral transgressors, unsightly untouchables, and *womanish* women.

When Jesus was **at the table**, there was a good chance that those who were invisible would be seen, those who were ignored or inaudible would be heard, and those who we're discarded would be accepted, when Jesus was at the table.

2. And into this space, a woman enters.

A woman came to him with an alabaster jar of very expensive perfume, which she poured on his head as he was reclining **at the table**.

Without a word or a knock, without an invitation or permission, without an announcement or a call to say, "I'm coming by." In comes this woman, asserting herself into the scene, demanding her place at the table just by her presence, and making for herself a way into Jesus' presence **at the table**.

Who was she?

Matthew allows the woman to remain anonymous. She has no name, no prior history, and no context clues about her identity. In Matthew, she could be anybody.

> She could've been the woman who touched his garment and received healing from her ceaseless bleeding.
> She could've been the woman who was delivered from her need for the constant affirmation and attention of men when she met Jesus at the well, and he gave her a deeper sense of purpose.
> She could've never even met Jesus, but merely heard about him and what he could do.
> She could be a woman like any anonymous mother with a reckless child.
> She could have been a sister with a dying brother whose only hope is Jesus cause she doesn't have any healthcare.
> She could have been a grandmother who has taken her grandbabies in to try to keep them from becoming sad statistics.
> Or, she could have been a wife who's lost her belief in marriage, doesn't know if she can trust her husband, or, if she even loves him anymore.

She could've been like any of these women who goes to Jesus, wondering, *if I just sit here and worship Jesus, will it make a difference in my situation?* Whoever she was and for whatever reason she was there, we know that she was there **at the table** to see Jesus.

3. But we also know that hers was a troubling presence to others in the room.

When the disciples and other guests saw this woman and her actions, they were indignant. "Why this waste," they asked? "This perfume could have been sold at a high price and the money given to the poor."

We're still **at the table**. With all of its politics and all of its stigmas, we're still **at the table**. The table is surrounded by men who were products of their contexts, and who are still looking to the table to rank themselves are at the table. However, Jesus is also there. **Jesus is still at the table.**

The truth is that anywhere that Jesus is should be a place of radical welcome. If Jesus can practice open table, why are we so intent on constructing boundaries and declaring who can and can't fit into them?

How are we good *stewards* of God's welcome toward us if we aren't extending it to others? What a waste of a welcome! In this nation, we have the nerve to declare human beings with lives, histories, stories, families and faith "illegal aliens." There are immigration laws that declare who "aliens" are, how long they can stay here, what they can do, and where they can go while they are here. These laws declare what kind of job they can work, and how often they must inform Uncle Sam of their address so he knows how to find them.

They must apply to carry Permanent Resident, or "Green" Cards. So, not only must they carry difference on their bodies, they must carry it in their wallets and pocketbooks, and be able to produce it to prove that they belong here. Or, live with the constant fear of "official removal," or deportation.

With no consideration for years of faithful service to the community or employment on their jobs or for the relationships they've developed or the homes they've built, they can be removed. Deported. Kicked out. Discarded. Here, we declare that we are the land of the free. We sing "God Bless America." Here, there are a lot of people who talk about God, but who have yet to receive the revelation of who God is. They have a short or non-existent historical memory.

Even in the Church and amongst the Body of Christ, those who say they have received the revelation. Somebody in here knows that you weren't always a card-carrying member of the Jesus club.

> Someone or something introduced you to Christ,
> > a relationship left you broken and weeping at the feet of Christ,
> > your family orphaned you to Christ,
> > you ended up crying out to Jesus and he took you in.
> > Jesus cradled your soul, accepted your worship, drew you close,
> > And now you have the nerve to shut the door on somebody else that needs him?

We are stuck on dictating the boundaries of belonging. It's the high school clique that you don't fit into because you're not black or white enough. It's the community club, the Boule, Jack and Jill, the Opera Society, the Scholars Guild that you are not "successful" or cultured enough to get in to. The sorority or fraternity that rejected you for whatever reason.

But maybe you aren't the exclusivist in the story. Maybe you're more like the woman who had an expensive gift, which she decided to give to Jesus. Maybe you're the one that's thinking about all the things you can do with all of the gifts and talents that you've been given, or things that you have acquired. You'd be thinking about how you can ball out, make more money off the money you have, how you can gain fame, get people to know you, "hype" yourself up with the gifts that God has given you.

> Oh yes, we lay our gifts on the altars of
> > Popularity and fame, hoping that somebody will notice us.
> > Facebook and hope that someone will send us a friend request.

Twitter and hope that someone will follow us.

And when they don't, it is easy to feel some kind of way. We live in an age where anyone can be their own hype man or hype woman, and it is easy to compare our journeys to what others are broadcasting about themselves. In May 2011, Pastor Steven Furtick tweeted, "One reason we struggle with insecurity is that we are comparing our behind-the-scenes to everyone else's highlight reel." We look at their highlight reels and believe that we are a waste, worthless. We compare ourselves so quickly and so harshly. As a result, we place ourselves on the sidelines and in the margins. We disqualify ourselves when we don't think that we have what it takes to be in the game.

This woman learned very quickly that it was a good thing that she lavished her gift on Jesus, because he *appreciated* it. This wasn't even her goal—to gain notoriety or even appreciation. She was there just to worship, to do something *kind* for Jesus on his way to the Cross.

This is a word for those of you in here who wonder if anyone notices your gifts, and who are waiting for that public affirmation. Waiting to be seen, to be heard, and to be appreciated. All around you, you see people being praised, and you know they ain't got the gift like you got it. You know they haven't consecrated their gifts before God or sold out to give God glory.

I encourage you to hold on. Don't cast your pearl of a gift before the swine of this world. Your gifts will make room for you! God does all things in God's perfect timing. When the time comes, God will unveil you and show you off to the world. So, wait for God to show you off. If you make it your mission to glorify God, and not to be seen, God will ensure that you are seen for the right reasons, by the right people, in the right places and at the right time.

4. Jesus will laud you.

"Why are you bothering this woman," Jesus asked. "She has done a beautiful thing to me. When she poured this perfume on my body, she did it to prepare me for my burial. I tell you the truth, wherever this gospel is preached throughout the world, what she has done will also be told, in memory of her."

So, she may have been worshipping to express thankfulness for something he'd already done. But, the scriptures say that this is a *prophetic act of worship*. This was worship for *what he is about to do*. She anointed him *in preparation* for his burial. She wasn't worshipping for what Jesus had already done. She worshipped him for that which she couldn't see, but that which she believed was coming. That's a right reason. That's why Jesus lauded her.

Additionally, although this woman might have been anonymous, she was no stranger. No stranger to Jesus would do this. But, to pour this love out, to risk humiliation the way she did—this was someone who'd had some sort of encounter with Jesus. This was not curious worship. This was not hearsay worship. This was an "*I know him for myself*" kind of worship. *I know him. I know he's good. I know he is worthy of this expensive gift.*

There had been some kind of exchange to make this woman want to come and worship Jesus before he was crucified. Because of what he'd done in the past, both for her and for others, she knew that was he was about to do had implications for her life. And because **he was at the table**, there was a way in for this woman to get into his presence and worship him.

At the heart of pure worship is gratitude, no matter what the act is. That's a right reason.

> When we worship by gathering, we are saying thank you for this village that covers me and cares for me.
> When we give monetarily, we give to thank God for giving us something to share.
> When we give our gifts to edify the kingdom of God, we give thanks that we are able to be a blessing.

Here, she was worshipping because she was grateful for what Jesus had done for her. If she's anything like us, maybe she was grateful that he *saw* her. That he *knew* her. That he *loved* her. He *moved* in her life and on her behalf.

Like Sybrina Fulton, a mother who lost her son, Trayvon Martin, to gun violence, and who recently saw a glimmer of the light of justice and said, "All we wanted was an arrest. Nothing more, nothing less, and we got it. And, I want to say thank you, Lord. Thank you, Jesus."

It is good news for all that Jesus is **still at the table**. Because he's **still at the table**, there's been a door opened to you. I'm wondering if there's one or two in here who know what it feels like to be blocked, to be prohibited, to be disallowed and unwelcomed.

Somebody somewhere told you "no."
Somebody told you "not you."
Somebody told you "not yet."
Somebody told you "not ever."

But what the enemy meant for evil, God turned it around for your good because **Jesus was at the table**.

A way was made for you because **Jesus was at the table**.

A door was opened for you because **Jesus was at the table**.

Well, the good news is that Jesus is still at the table today!

If you're in need of something from him, come to the table.

If you're in need of healing and deliverance, come to the table.

If you're in need of a turnaround in your life and your faith, come.

Jesus is still at the table!

If you're looking for a way in, if the door has been closed to you elsewhere, come.

Jesus is still at the table!

If you're wondering if justice is still a possibility, you need to know that the answer is yes, because Jesus is still at the table!

If you're wondering if he can use you, to serve this present age, to help usher in the kingdom of God, come.

Jesus is still at the table!

And if you're grateful for what he's done, just like the woman who poured out her oil, and you just want to pour out some praise for him, come!
Jesus is still at the table!

Note
1. Nathan Mitchell, Eucharist as Sacrament of Initiation, Forum Essays, 2 (Chicago: Liturgy Training Publications, 1994), 89-90.

DON'T MISS THE KINGDOM

MARK 10:17-21 (NRSV)

Preached June 2015 at the closing session of The Justice Conference, Chicago, IL.

It had been a really, really, good life. This man had arrived. He was successful by every worldly standard. He had a lot of money, and of course, a lot of money afforded him a lot of things:

> A nice place to live in, decorated to the nines.
> A nice vehicle with rims and detail.
> A lot of people who loved to be around him.
> An impressive job that paid him well, and that provided him with great health coverage, glamorous trips, and access to the rich and famous.

Yes, by all worldly standards, his was a good life.

But, something happened. Maybe he found himself facing a quarter-life or a mid-life crisis, or maybe he'd had some life-altering experience, and the question of, "what is it all for?" began to weigh heavily upon his spirit. Yes, he had a great life, but in the few quiet moments of honesty that he'd spent with himself, he began to feel as if all that he had worked for wasn't leading him to the peace, contentment, and happiness that he had hoped for. All of his life, he had worked to get here.

> Went to the right school, took the right classes, and joined the right fraternity.
> Got the right internship and the right mentors, and landed the right job.
> Sacrificed anything, sometimes even his own values, shook the right hands, wore the right suits, and got the right promotions.
> Worked his way from the bottom to the top, got there and found that the top was, at best, just okay.

After all this "work," he was beginning to see that he worked too much to cultivate real relationships, but he *had* to work to keep his prestigious job. The so-called friends that he did have were always around when the party was going on and when dinner was on him, but when he needed someone to talk to or feel connected to, there was no one to be found. Fly-by-night relationships gave him the façade of love and romance, but he'd ultimately ended up alone most of the time because he had trouble committing to one person. There was only so much satisfaction that could come from luxury trips and shopping sprees. Yes, after all that he had done to get here, he was finding that "here" was a lonely, isolating and unforgiving place.

Anybody ever been there? Worked so hard to get somewhere and found that it wasn't all that you thought it would be?

> Gotten into the school, gotten the job,
> Gotten the popularity, the fame and the following,
> Gotten the guy, gotten the girl, the relationship and even the marriage,
> Signed the deal, gotten the "stuff" and the "big opportunity . . ."

Only to find that it really wasn't all that after all?

Has anyone gotten to the place, reached the goal, arrived to the destination and discovered that you'd placed a whole lot of energy in something that could only satisfy you so much. You caught a case of misguided expectations and misplaced priorities.

Well, don't beat yourself up. We've all been there. And in this text, this young ruler is there right now. Yeah, he had a good life, but it had been a long life of hustling to get a lifestyle that didn't fulfill him on the inside. Because lately, he's been waking up in the morning, feeling lonely and wondering, "why am I doing this again?" There was no elevated purpose for his money, his stuff, and even his life.

He was suffering from a crisis of identity, or a crisis of "why?" He didn't know the "why" behind his waking up and working so hard, and getting up the next morning and doing it over, and over, and over again. These crises had become unbearable. They had become urgent. They had begun to cost him his sleep and his peace of mind.

So much so that when he heard that Jesus was coming through, the Bible says that he "ran up" to Jesus and "knelt before him."

> What an unfamiliar and humble posture for such an "important" man to assume.

This is the thing about the presence of Jesus: when he arrives, atmospheres shift and people are changed. In the presence of Jesus, true character is revealed. And today, this rich ruler was beginning to see that even though he had a lot of money, he was still deeply impoverished and completely needy. He needed answers, so he asked Jesus a question: "Good Teacher, what must I do to inherit eternal life?"

And that, my brothers and sisters, is a loaded question. Within the question itself, the man is expressing that this life *can't* be all there is; there must be more! "There has got to be more to life, more to even me, than this. How, Jesus, can I obtain it?"

And tonight, I've been sent to the one or two people in this room who are living with the same anxiety: *there's got to be more to life than this*. I've been sent to the two or three of you who've got the same question: *what do I have to do to obtain eternal life, and to ensure that my life has meaning and relevance beyond myself and beyond my job, my stuff, and my time on earth?*

The first thing that I want to say is that this is a great question. As anxiety-inducing and frustrating as it is, this is a great question. And God is looking for a few people who are brave enough to ask this question because there are some things that are going on this world that are breaking the heart of God. And I believe that God's heart will be mended by those who want their lives to have greater significance.

This is a great question with a complex answer. To obtain eternal life, and relevance beyond yourself and your stuff, make Jesus, and doing the work of Jesus, the center of your life. That's what he told the rich young ruler. "Sell all you have and follow me." In other words, *show me that I matter most and then come follow me. And then, come help me with the work I came to do. Unstick yourself from your stuff.*

When a Black or brown person is killed by a rogue cop every 28 hours, there is work for you to do.

Unstick yourself from your stuff and follow Christ.

When people still don't have their daily bread, decent housing, or access to education, there is work for you to do.

Unstick yourself from your stuff.

When there are so many brokenhearted people, God needs some heart-menders, who are willing to get to work mending the brokenness and eradicating the injustice of the world.

Unstick yourself from your stuff and get to work.

Asking this question of purpose signifies to God that you want an assignment and to be used to do God's work. Maybe you know what your assignment is, and you just came here for some motivation. But, maybe you don't know, and you came to The Justice Conference to get some clarity about what God is asking you to do. Anybody ready for an assignment? Good.

However, there are a few caveats—a few warnings that I need to give you.

1. You need to grow up.

If you want to know the why of your life, *you've got to look beyond your life*. The call of God is meant to make you stand taller, stretch you wider, and take you deeper than you think you can go. In order to unstick ourselves from our stuff, we must first grow up.

The first thing that Jesus does in this text is answer the rich young man's question with a question: "You know the commandments?" And the five commandments that Jesus lifted are unique because these five have primarily to do with one's relationship to other *people*:

1. Don't cheat on *people* you love and with whom you are in covenant.
2. Don't kill *people*.
3. Don't take what belongs to other *people*.
4. Don't lie on *people*.
5. Respect the *people* who birthed you into the world.

Jesus lifted these five commandments, and other *people* are at the heart of these. This makes sense coming from the mouth of Jesus because if you look at the record of Jesus' life and how he spent his time, there are a few occurrences of him going to the temple, teaching and having debates with the religious leaders. But, 90% of the Gospels present a Jesus who was all about *people*. He was constantly moving around trying to be with *the people*,

Connecting and correcting people,
Reaching and teaching people,
Announcing and embodying the coming of the love of God to forgotten people,
Building a prophetic sub-community, a movement powered by radical love for marginalized people.

It turns out that not only does the rich ruler know these commandments, but he has also been keeping them his whole life.

Right here, in Mark, it says that Jesus "loved him." He saw that the man was making an attempt to live righteously. His heart was in the right place. But, it's not enough to have a heart that's in the right place if you're not pushing the world to a better place. So, Jesus doesn't discount him, but he pushes him to *grow up*.

He challenges him to push himself beyond himself and beyond what he's so proud to morally claim. Not to say that keeping these five very anthropological commandments is easy, but if your understanding of Jesus and the Bible is anchored in simply keeping commandments, you can spend time keeping them, and be blinded to the fact that you are not *living beyond the commandments*, which is what Jesus came to show us how to do. You can tell yourself, "I'm a good person. I don't harm anyone. I'm doing what the Bible says to do."

But following Jesus requires that we *grow up*. It means that every now and then, Jesus will come to us and force us to ask a critical question: "Am I going to stop at being a good person or will I also do God's work?" To follow Jesus, to co-labor with Jesus in transforming this world, you've got to be about the things that Jesus is about. Jesus has requirements of us. They are designed to stretch us. They are designed to open us up to the discomfort that produces change in us and around us. They are designed to induce anguish at unjust world conditions.

God's requirements are designed to challenge us, to call us up a little higher, to destroy our self-imposed limitations and the glass ceilings that are above our heads. God's requirements require us to put our childish ways behind us. They are designed to subvert our selfishness, to push against our fear, and to finally call OUR egos into submission to the will and word of God.

Your mission will require more of you. Your assignment will make great demands of your time, and if you're distracted, you won't complete your mission. Your assignment will require your heart, and if you have not been about the work of healing your own heart, you can't go out and heal the hearts of others. Your mission will require maturity, and you, my brother, my sister, will need to start making some new decisions—some hard decisions. Some inconvenient decisions, everyday! You can start today by deciding, "I'm going to GROW UP."

> I'm not going to be content with where I've been.
> I won't be satisfied with what I know.
> I will stop wasting my time and energy.
> I will stop being so self-centered.
> I will stop thinking that it's enough to cry over injustice.
> I will press on to do the work of the God.

2. Jesus will challenge you to become Kingdom-minded.

Not only will Jesus let you know that you have to grow up, but he will also challenge you. The challenge will almost always have to do with what matters most to you. It will always have to do with that which makes you most comfortable and most secure, and is the greatest source of your *privilege* in this world.

Jesus was serious. "Sell everything. Give 100% of your profits away; don't even keep a dollar for yourself. Once you've done this, come and follow me." It's interesting that this rich young ruler said that he had kept all the commandments since his youth. Well, now he gets a chance to prove it. Jesus did not name it, but the FIRST commandment says, "Thou shall have no other God before me." The young man thought he had kept all the commandments since his youth. But when he was told to sell everything and give everything away, the Bible says, "He went away sad, because he was very rich." In other words, he had placed another god before God; his money was his first God. He failed at the first commandment.

You have failed in life if all you are is what you've earn, what you amassed, and what you own. It does not matter if you have a regular pew at the church and can regularly be found in it. It does not matter if you give to great causes, if God is not the center of your life. Why? Because you will never become consistently and thoroughly kingdom-minded if your greatest concern and your greatest love is that which is materialistic.

Jesus was trying to get the rich young man to become Kingdom-minded. He knew he was tethered to his stuff. He wanted to grow him up and move him to being Kingdom-minded. I'm not talking about a militaristic, triumphalist Kingdom that is taken by force and violence in the name of the great "King Jesus." That kind of kingdom would be too close in resemblance to the kingdoms of this world.

There are all types of systems and organizations built on the assumption of power and the execution of power. These systems are often built on faulty foundations of racism, patriarchy, and nationalism. These systems are built on the ideas that some people are human and some are not, and that some people deserve a decent life and some do not. Dr. Cornel West taught us last night that this kind of "Kingdom" lies at the heart of American "democracy," which was built on the backs of slaves and established to the exclusion of their lives.

I don't know about you, but when I turned on my television last August and I saw military tanks lining the streets of Ferguson, Missouri; when I saw tear gas being released on everyday, innocent people just trying to be heard; when I saw police officers who looked more like soldiers, and peaceful protests being construed as riots and protesters as thugs, I saw all over again the manifested kingdom of darkness. Let me remind you, just in case you have forgotten, that the event that instigated these protests was the murder of an 18-year-old young man by the name of Michael Brown, Jr. And, just in case you've forgotten the story, let me remind you that on the morning of August 4, 2014, after Mike Brown *allegedly* stole some cigarettes from a Ferguson convenience store, he and his friend were stalked by Officer Darren Wilson. An altercation ensued, in which Mike Brown was shot twelve times by Wilson. He was unarmed.

Months later, in November, it was decided by a grand jury that Wilson would not be even be indicted. Soon thereafter, in a televised interview with George Stephanopoulos, Wilson admitted that he was afraid for his life because Mike Brown was big and black and looked "demonic." Therefore, he claimed that he killed Brown out of self-defense. He admitted that he didn't regret it because he did what he was trained to do and that he would, in fact, do it again.

Unless you've been living under a rock, you're aware that a movement is going on. It's often referred to as the Black Lives Matter Movement. It's broken out all over the country. Simultaneously, Black lives continue to be taken by law enforcement officials. Let me do a brief roll call, just for your information:

Tamir Rice, age 12, playing with a toy gun in a park in Cleveland, shot dead upon the assumption that his gun was real even after a 911 caller, whose message was never relayed to the police, said "It looks like it might be a toy." The officer fired his weapon *two seconds* after arriving at the scene.

Eric Garner was selling loose cigarettes on a corner in New York, perhaps to make ends meet at home. He was suffocated—on video—by New York police officers, and with his last breath, he gave us the war cry of, "I Can't Breathe."

> Tanisha Anderson, 37
> Rekia Boyd, 22
> Freddie Gray, 25
> Walter Scott, 50

And this is just a very short, short list.

In his book, *The Prophetic Imagination*, Walter Brueggemann writes extensively about the Kingdom of God, not so much as a place, but as a shift in social conditions that creates a new world. An alternative consciousness shared by an alternative thinking community. A way of living that stands in direct contrast to the dominant structures and oppressive people. He writes that in Jesus and in the movement that he created, the kingdom of God was enfleshed. According to Brueggemann, the birth and the life of Jesus accomplished two things: prophetic criticism of the old ways and the dominant powers, and prophetic energizing through the creation of new realities.

The Jesus Movement (which is the Kingdom Movement) could be summarized in one verse: Luke 7:22—*"the blind receive their sight, the lame walk, lepers are cleansed, and the deaf hear, the dead are raised up, the poor have good news preached to them."*

It was a movement of restoration and preservation of *people's lives*.

And, so, there is a parallel here between the kingdom of God and the Black Lives Matter movement. When Jesus told the rich ruler that it would be difficult for him to enter the Kingdom because he was rich, it was another way of saying that his wealth was the very reason why others were poor. His wealth, comfort, and privilege were the reasons why others lived in disenfranchisement, poverty and political vulnerability. *He couldn't come up into the Kingdom, into the movement, if his privileges were harming the very people the movement existed to serve.* No!

The people didn't need his tax-deductible donations. The people didn't need him to support poverty legislation while also supporting the NRA. The people didn't need him to join a march on one day under the influence of his "wealth guilt," and then leave to return to his oppressive practices the next day.

No. They needed someone who was willing to work with them for their liberation as long as it took for their liberation to come. They needed someone who was willing to struggle until struggle was no more. Matter of fact, they needed someone who *knew* that this struggle is OURS, and it is for OUR liberation.

They needed someone who would commit to the movement. Give up their comfort and get on this Love Train. Give up their privilege because they believe that a more just world for God's children is more important than a comfortable and cushy world for the rich. *If you're going to be committed to the Kingdom of God, you've got to get out of your addiction to convenience.* Commitment and convenience often negate one another. On your mission, you won't always be able to have both because commitment is often *inconvenient*.

Jesus tells this man, you can't enter the Kingdom with the thing you rely on to save you. I don't know what it is in your case, but in his case, it was his money. People were dying in *his backyard* and he didn't *do* anything about it. Maybe it was more comforting for him to pretend that it wasn't happening. Writing his check to Africa warmed his heart and made him feel good about himself. His money provided him with comfort and security. It endowed him with the power of *charitable disposability*—the ability to give away his money to charitable causes, with no real cost to him. Jesus' request turned his privilege on its head by telling him: *grow up*, sell everything you own, give the money away, and then come follow me. Show me you really ultimately want to follow me by working with me for the least of these. Learn what it feels like to walk a day in the shoes of the poor. Feel the desperation from not having enough money to eat or enough power to change your condition. Feel that first—and then come.

Justice movements should be people-powered. But, let me say this: there is no need for people to be part of the movement with their body—you know—show up to the protest when they can—if they're not in the movement with their heart. And sometimes, to be in the movement with your heart, you've got to divest, release, give up and put away some privileges.

This Black Lives Matter Movement is going on, and perhaps you've wondered, "how can I get involved?" Here are a couple of things that you should check on before you show up to the protest:

Write down what it that gives you the most access, the most comfort, the most power in this world? For example:

I'm white,
I'm heterosexual,
I'm wealthy,
I'm a male,
I have a clearly identifiable gender, all of my limbs are properly functioning, I'm sufficiently educated, I come from a family from which I inherited wealth, I never had to apply for US Citizenship, etc.

1. **Acknowledge** that you have this privilege. Before you get uncomfortable or start crying about it, just name it. Sit with it.
2. **Repent** for the ways you've abused this or used it for your own gain or the gain of people like you.
3. **Realize** the ways that your privilege creates the conditions for someone else's oppression.

4. **Record** the benefits that your privilege provides you simply because you have it.
5. **Pray** for a burden.

Because it's only when you're burdened that you will find yourself running to the feet of Jesus, bowing down and asking "what must I do?" A burden is something that weighs heavily on your heart.

> A burden will keep you up at night.
> A burden will take hold of your insides and not let go until you do something.
> A burden will stir your spirit and move it to lament.
> A burden will steal your peace and frustrate you when you see conditions that don't seem to change.
> A burden will put anguish in your soul and ultimately force you to ask, "What must I do?"

A burden will also get you energized and make you strategize. Making coalitions and building networks with people with the same burden.

> A burden will get you to work until you see some shifts taking place.
> A burden will prod you, poke you, push you until you cannot tolerate your own apathy and complacency.
> A burden will make you feel powerless sometimes, but it will convince you that you *still* have to do *something*.
> A burden might totally shake up your life, but a burden will make you more like Jesus!

Pray for a burden! And write down what it is, now.
A burden for the distressed.
A burden for the poor.
A burden for the monetized bodies of girls and boys, men and women in the human trafficking industry.
A burden for Black and Brown bodies killed by cops.

A burden for the men and women locked up in the Prison Industrial System.

A burden for the disabled, including those made so by going to war.

A burden for the depressed, the lonely, and the broken.

Anybody got a burden? Carrying a burden that burdens the heart of God? That's good news.

3. Choose

Finally, there's good news for all of us tonight. In the text, Jesus was hard on the man; he was brutally honest that the building the Kingdom of God is not for the faint of heart and that following him will cost you something. But, after this, he extended an invitation to the rich ruler, and it's an invitation that still stands today.

> *"and then, come, follow me."*

Being a follower of Jesus goes beyond getting "saved" and going to church. That's easy. It's sad because this is the routine of many Christians, or "Church people." And, it stops there. There's no transformation, no growth, no deep theological inquiry, no interface with the God of Justice in prophetic worship, no getting beyond the walls of the church. It's scary because to a lot of people, this is all they think of when they hear "Christian," someone who goes to church and is really good at judging and condemning other people in the name of Jesus. The late Rev. William Augustus Jones said, "It's a sad thing to get so close to the shore and drown in shallow water. *Don't miss the Kingdom* for shallow reasons." **The present age isn't in need of any more Christians.** We need followers of Jesus who go where Jesus would go, who try to do what Jesus did, and try to do the greater things that he said we would do. And if you ask a follower of Jesus, they will tell you that this hurts and it's not easy, and that it is not shallow. Being a follower of Jesus requires that we do deep work in deep waters.

I don't want to valorize my journey or myself, but this story strikes me. When Peter turns to Jesus and says, "Jesus, we've given up our homes, everything to follow you," I can really relate. Let me testify. I left home at the age of 18, and I haven't lived there since. My ministry has taken me all over the country, but never to the places where my family live and where I identify as "home." God only knows how much it would mean to me to be released back to San Antonio or Atlanta, just to be close to my family and enjoy some warmth. But, Jesus hasn't led me home. If I go where he hasn't led me, I've no longer chosen to follow him. I made my mind up to follow Jesus, no matter what, and despite living without the thing I desire most, my family, Jesus has given me a lot of new family right where I'm at. He's taking care of me.

The best part of the story comes when Jesus gives his disciples a promise: "Truly, I tell you, there is no one who has left house or spouse or siblings or parents or children, for the sake of the kingdom of God, who will not get back very much more in this age, and in the age to come, eternal life."

He's clear. You've got to make some hard choices. He is also clear that when you make the hard choices, he will not abandon you. He sees the sacrifice, and he honors it. He honors it so much so that he's willing to give you very much more, including eternal life in his Kingdom. Don't miss this Kingdom.

PUBLIC DISPLAYS OF AFFECTION

JOHN 13:3-8 (NRSV)

Preached Maundy Thursday, 2015 at Trinity United Church of Christ, Chicago, IL.

Everyone in this room has had the experience of being in a relationship with someone whose words and ways did not always correspond. You'd hear one thing from their mouth, but you'd see something different in their behavior. You might have heard, "I love you, I love you, baby, I love you," but saw that they didn't take the time to spend time with you. You might have heard, "You're doing a great job, we've got our eyes on you for the promotion," but you look up and it's been five years, and those same eyes that were on you have overlooked you too many times to count. You might have heard, "Your game is on point, it's time we put you in the game," but you're still warming the bench, waiting for your two minutes of playing time.

Because we have all had this experience, I am going to assume that we all know the anxiety that can come from this situation. It is confusing when the message spoken with words and the message spoken through deeds are in conflict. Eventually, wisdom hits, you get smarter, and you get to the point where you realize that actions really do speak louder than words. You learn to look not to what some people say about you, but to how they treat you.

In John 13, we find ourselves coming to the end of Jesus' life and ministry on earth. The chapter is the first of four chapters widely considered to be his "Departure Discourse," or, his teachings on how his disciples and followers, and eventually the Church, were to conduct themselves upon his departure. We see him in close and private quarters with his disciples, imparting last minute teachings about important things, such as "not letting our hearts be troubled" and "waiting on the Advocate, the Spirit of God." But, before Jesus ever says a word in this "discourse," Jesus does something. Before he ever said a word, Jesus displays everything that is on his heart to say. While Jesus was full of words of instruction, his first matter of business on his way to the Cross was to *show* his love for the people of God, to publicly display his affection.

The text tells us that Jesus changed his clothes. He removed his robe and tied a towel around his waist, so as to take on, to embody, to become a servant to his disciples. In other words, as a public display of affection, Jesus was willing to reverse his role in their lives.

Foot washing was an act of hospitality in the ancient world. At a time when sandals were the most popular footwear, a host would often provide two things to their guests upon entry into their home: a basin and a towel for washing their feet. And, they would provide a servant to actually wash their feet. It was a rare occasion when the host himself, or herself, would wash the feet of their guests.

Up until this point, the disciples called him "Lord;" they called him "Teacher;" and they called him "Master." But, the disciples never knew him as "Servant." The performance of this humble act, this self-effacing act, was saved for those whose social status as servant, was less likely to induce any anxiety or embarrassment about the condition of a guest's feet. With a servant, it wasn't necessary to go get a pedicure before they washed your feet. With a servant, you didn't have to worry about how your feet were smelling or how rough and cracked your heels were. You didn't have think about the corns and bunions that resulted from wearing shoes that you know never fit your feet. With a servant, you never had to worry about how your feet would convey about your status, because surely your status as "guest" was higher than theirs as "servant."

This may explain Peter's anxiety when it was his turn to have his feet washed. Having seen Jesus washing and drying the feet of his disciples, he got nervous. "Lord, are *you* about to wash *my* feet?" Peter had been walking with Jesus and ministering with Jesus long enough to have gotten used to the attention being on the needs of others, the infirmities of others, and the issues of others. His position as a disciple had always meant that he was the one serving, not the one being served.

Moreover, it was far less invasive to simply touch someone and heal them of their sickness. It was far less vulnerable to be the one breaking the bread and fish to feed the masses. None of this, nor any of the other things they'd witness Jesus do, was this personally intrusive. "You want to wash my feet?" Peter asked.

So here in this scene, we have Jesus reversing his role as Messiah and becoming Servant. And we have Simon Peter, the servant who is clearly uncomfortable with being served.

Peter raises a question to all of us tonight, "We know Jesus as Teacher, Messiah, God with us. Some of us here, sitting in this sanctuary, even know Jesus as Savior. But what would it mean for us to know Jesus as servant?"

Well, the answer is in the text, in verse 8, "Unless, I wash you, you have no share in me." In other words, *"Peter, you have to take your sandals off and show me your feet. Stop hiding them. Stop hiding the dirt under your nails, the roughness of your skin and the odor that has built up from your journey today. In order for me to wash you, to serve you, you've got to show me what you don't want me to see." You've got trust me that I'm not here to judge you but to serve you, to wash you, and make you more suitable for my service."*

Every now and then, we servants of God, have to take a moment and stop serving long enough to be served.

> Whether it's a broken spirit that you're hiding behind a smile,
> Whether it's a disappointed heart that you hide behind dutifully singing in the choir,
> Whether it's a dark, cloudy, and depressed mind that you hide behind as you sit on the Deacon Board,

Whether it's that you were victimized in the dark of the night years ago, and you're hiding your pain as you usher at the church doors,

Jesus is standing in this room right now saying, *"I cannot completely be your Savior. I want to be, but you've got to stop, sit down, and show me the broken, rotten, festering and odorous thing that you've been hiding. You've got to let me see it.* **Let me inspect it with my eyes, so that I can wash you with my hands.***"*

These are the *same hands* that healed the blind.
The *same hands* that delivered the demon-possessed.
The *same hands* that touched the infirmed and gave them a new beginning,
and the *same hands* that took nails for your salvation
are the same hands that want to wash you.

Wash you of your rage.
Wash you of your grief.
Wash you of your self-hate.
Wash you of your trauma.
Wash you of your stank and your funk.

But you've got to stop hiding long enough for me to wash you.
If we allow Jesus see us and wash us, then we can be healed and become whole. Ultimately, we can be empathetic enough to accept those who society finds the least acceptable!

When we allow Jesus to wash us, the people whom we attempt to serve become more recognizable because we see their pain not as unique, not as untouchable, nor too overwhelming to address. We begin to see human beings whose lives are not so unlike our own.

No one wants to live on the streets and tell the world that they're addicted to harmful substances. No one wants to go to a battered women's shelter with their children and admit they hooked up with men who were of adult age, but who were childish in their actions. No one wants to stand in the unemployment line and let it be known that they were fired and need help making ends meet. No middle-aged adult wants to return to school and have people think it took them forever to get their act together, to figure out the right career, or to just grow up.

These are secrets that people would rather keep hidden. They would rather live in secrecy and in the shadows with their shame and pain. When we can tell the truth about our doubts, our self-hatred, our confusion, our lack of self-care, our lack of commitment to our people, our stinginess, our manipulation, our lack of courage, our unwillingness to change, and our judgmental attitudes, then Jesus can wash us. Then, we can begin to serve and love others, the way that Jesus serves and loves us. The public display of affection that Jesus humbly showed to his disciples becomes contagious. It touches and moves our hearts, our hands, our feet, and perhaps even our wallets. We have the urge to serve, because we have been served by the Savior!

Once you know that he cared enough to serve you and to wash you—*all of you*—your only response can be a heart overflowing with gratitude that leads you to public displays of affection, acts of service and love to your brother and your sister. A song sums this up well:

I was sinking deep in sin, far from the peaceful shore,
Very deeply stained within, sinking to rise no more,
But the Master of the sea heard my despairing cry,
From the waters lifted me, now safe [and washed] am I.

Love lifted me!
Love lifted me!
When nothing else could help,

Love lifted me!
All my heart to Him I give, ever to Him I'll cling,
In His blessed presence live, ever His praises sing,
Love so mighty and so true, merits my soul's best songs,
Faithful, loving service, too, *to Him belongs.*

HERE I AM TO WORSHIP

EXODUS 3:1-6 (NRSV)

Preached November 2015, The Dangerous Act of Worship Revival, Arnett Chapel AME Church, Chicago, IL

I was about 16 years old when I boarded a bus with about 50 other teenagers, leaving San Antonio to go to Houston for a youth conference. Six months prior, my mother joined a new church, New Creation Christian Fellowship. This was one of my first encounters with the youth ministry. I don't recall knowing many people, but I do remember thinking that this trip would be a good opportunity to get to know them. After all, this was our new church, and like a lot of Black folks, we would be spending a lot of time at this church. So, I took the road trip to attend this conference with these teens, and the very enthusiastic youth pastor, Elder Campbell. I liked Elder Campbell because he had a passion for Christ and this energy that made being a Christian seem fun. In addition, his discernment game was on point, and he could read any of us after just a few moments of staring into our faces. Over the three hours of the trip, I realized that it was his witness that drew me to this conference. I could actually get down with the Jesus that he represented.

I could never be ready for what was waiting for me in Houston. I don't remember a lot of the preaching, and I don't remember a lot of people doing a lot of any kind of talking. I do remember the worship. I should back up here to say that I have always been a "church girl," one who was practically birthed onto the pews. As the granddaughter of a Baptist pastor, the daughter of an avid Baptist and an avid Roman Catholic, my family's Sundays were always full and robust with worship. I'd known Black church my whole life. I heard a lot about God, seen a lot of baptisms and Lord's Suppers, and had even been confirmed in the Catholic Church. But, I was far from being a Christian and even further from being a follower of Jesus. Yet, somewhere in the beautiful matrix of music, exhortation, and stillness at the youth conference, I came a little bit closer.

I should also insert here that I'm from a charismatic background. Crying, shouting, prophesying, and yes, even speaking in other tongues, were commonplace in my upbringing, and they mark a place of faith and surrender that I never want to leave. It was there at that conference in that hotel ballroom, caught in that sonic, aesthetic, and ambient matrix of mysticism, that God met me in a real way, as my own tears flooded my face and my own shouts of surrender filled my vicinity. I remember my heart being so full and so peaceful, as I decided that I wanted to be a Christian and spend the rest of my life trying to follow Jesus. Indeed, it was fitting that this conference was called "Face to Face" because that's where I felt I ended up: face to face with a decision to surrender totally to Christ.

In this evening's text, we find Moses, the great liberator of his people, before he was the great liberator of his people. Here, he's merely a shepherd. He's a sheepherder, working on the side of Mount Sinai for his father-in-law Jethro. Up to this point, Moses had come of age under some curious conditions. First, there was the edict of male child infanticide that was issued before his birth. The edict that caused his mother to place him in a basket and send him upstream, because rather than the certainty of killing her child, she preferred the *what if* of sending him up the river alive. Then, there was his growth and development in the home of Pharaoh— the king who was responsible for the enslavement of Moses' people.

Finally, there was the incident that caused Moses to run. After witnessing an Egyptian beating a Hebrew, he became enraged and secretly killed the oppressor. The following day, he became more enraged when he saw two Hebrews fighting each other, and discovered that his secret murder had not been as secret as he thought.

He was enraged over the condition of his people being oppressed, from without and within. He was livid, to the point of murder, at their systemic enslavement and the disposability of their lives in the eyes of Egyptian authorities. And, he was also enraged to see that somewhere along the line, the Hebrews imbibed and internalized this message. They became self-hating and began to inflict violence upon each other. Somewhere in his heart Moses heard the cry, "Hebrew lives matter! My people matter!" This call from within caused him to rise to action. Despite having been raised in the home of his oppressor, he never stopped identifying with his own people.

Moses' example lets us know that it doesn't matter how far you get from the 'hood you were raised in or the people who look like you, it is never okay to sell them out. It is never okay to turn your back on your own people, especially if you are in a position to help them. To the Ben Carsons, Raven Symones, and Don Lemons of the world, watch out! There will come a day when you will face dispossession from the kingdoms and systems of this world, and you will have to face the fact that you are Black like the rest of us, and what are you going to do that day? People such as these may want to take a cue from the Moses' of this world; because despite whatever power, authority, or clout they may think they have, we would never entrust our lives or our liberations into their hands for, in the words of Drake, "y'all ain't never loved us." And in the words of Cornel West, "You cannot lead the people if you don't love the people. You cannot save the people if you do not serve the people." So perhaps, Moses was well qualified to lead and liberate his people because he loved them.

His love led him to do something for which he could have been killed. Yet, before he could get caught, he ran away and made a life for himself. And, now here he is in tonight's text, tending to Jethro's flock on the side of Sinai. He is working. He is busy. He is occupied in this moment because he doesn't want to lose any of his father-in-law's sheep. As he is working, as he is busy and occupied, he sees a curious site that interrupts his busy schedule. The text says: "There the angel of the Lord appeared to him in flames of fire from within a bush." Moses saw that though the bush was on fire, it did not burn up. So, he decides, *I've never seen anything like this before! Let me get closer and see why the bush is not burning up.* This sight suddenly interrupted Moses' work. His curiosity drew him to see what this could be, and how it could be happening.

I want to suggest that worship is an activity of the curious. The curious are those who are not so wedded to the routine and their rubrics, their structures and their programs that they can't go off script for a moment, and see just what would happen if they stopped what they were doing to get closer to the strange sight of the Spirit. I get tired of being in services when I can feel that God has something different in mind than what is printed in the bulletin, but the leaders and the people resist the shift in the atmosphere because it's not what they are used to. They don't know what to do in God's presence because they rarely spend time there. I even get tired of myself when I feel God calling me into worship, and I choose sleep or Facebook or whatever instead.

Worship—not church, not liturgy—but intimate, vulnerable, and divinely unfolding time in the holy presence of the Lord is inconvenient. God often calls us into God's presence when we least expect it, and often calls us to stay there until God is done speaking. It can disrupt our schedules and it can mess with our routines, but I think that's the very point of it. If we allow God to mess with our schedules and routines and what we are used to seeing, we are also allowing God to mess with our hearts. We are allowing God to speak to, break, mold, mend, and transform our hearts.

Perhaps this is one reason why worship is so dangerous: you cannot be in the presence of God and remain the same. You cannot be in the presence of the Holy and be cool with your sin, your stains, and your stank. When God gives you a glimpse of God's Self, God is also giving you a glimpse of who you can be. So *why* would you want to stay the same? Worship is for those who are open to the change, the transformation, and the metamorphosis of God taking place in your life. Worship *invites* change. Worship is for those who are curious enough to get closer to the unusual and to engage the unscripted. Worship is for those who might even be a little wild at heart, who rather than running away from the unknown and strange presence of God, they want to know more about it, and so they come closer.

Moses decided that this sight of a bush that was on fire, but wasn't burning up, deserved his full attention. He could have merely observed, taken note of how interesting it was, and kept on herding. But he went closer, and God saw it. "When the Lord saw that Moses had gone over to look, God called to him . . ." Moses' response pleased God's heart. "Hmmm," said God in that moment. "It worked. I got his attention." God got Moses' attention so much so that he stopped what he was doing and went closer. It was an act of desire, an act of his agency and his own volition. Here was a choice that he made to draw closer to that strange presence. It was either a "yes," a "maybe," or even a "what if" that drew him closer. The fact remains that he made the conscientious decision to come closer to a movement of God.

Worship is a choice we make. In a world where so many other things are competing for our attention and for our affection, worship is a choice we make. This is why I get so infuriated by "liturgical cultural critics" who critique Black worship and charismatic worship as mindless. Do they not know that when we worship, it is a decision that we make with our minds? Have they not heard that worshipping God with vigor and with strength and with passion is a choice that has sustained us amidst centuries of cultural and social bondage?

Furthermore, God doesn't want our worship out of obligation or duty or coercion. God wants us to worship because *we want to worship*. Worship is an act of love. It is intimate, and it is sacrificial. No one wants to twist your arm to love him or her, or to spend time with him or her. That isn't love. That's domination and control, and we know that this pseudo-love often leads to violence. While worship may be dangerous, worship is not meant to be violent. You ought to want to worship God. Is there anybody here who *wants* to draw closer and worship the Lord?

Moses went closer, and when God saw it, God took it as an opportunity to talk to Moses. So God called out his name: "Moses, Moses!" Moses replied, "Here I am." With these three words, "Here I am," Moses' life was set on a divinely appointed, divinely orchestrated trajectory. This moment was the most pivotal of all up to this point in the narrative of Moses' life. By coming closer to the fire and surrendering with "Here I am," he submitted to the will and plan of God. He came when he was called, and he presented himself as willing and available to hear whatever the Lord wanted to say to him. When he went closer and submitted, what happened?

1. He received instruction.

He received instruction. "Do not come any closer. Take off your shoes, for this is holy ground." If you're ever in need of an instruction as to what to do in life, get into the presence of God. Sometimes, we become so overwhelmed by the bigger picture, when all we need are instructions on what to do next. God essentially told Moses, "Before you do anything else, take off your shoes. Don't worry about what is coming after this step. Take this step, and let the next one be revealed when it's time to take it."

"Take off your shoes" is not just a pragmatic instruction. The directive let Moses clearly know that he was in the presence of the Presence. The act was designed to show respect and humility. God has standards for our behavior when we are in God's presence. What have you taken off in the presence of God? There are some things that we absolutely, positively need to take off before entering the presence of God to worship. We need to remove things such as our pride, our false identities, our selfish ambitions and self-serving agendas. Things such as our apathy, our prejudices, our biases. This baggage cannot stand in God's presence, and if you cannot lay them down, ask for God's help.

2. He received an introduction.

God had already revealed God's Self to Moses' ancestors. These ancestors had known God when they walked the earth, but now, it was time for Moses to have an opportunity to know God, to have his own walk with God. As he came into God's presence, a wonderful revelation of God was given.

Hello, Moses. I am the God of your father, the God of Abraham, the God of Isaac, and the God of Jacob. But, allow me to introduce myself to you. I want to show you who I am, in a way that will make you understand who I am. It will be a new way to you and to your generation. But, before I make you great among all people, I need to know that you desire to know me, that you will honor me, that you will acknowledge my sovereignty.

And at this introduction, Moses turns his face away. My research reveals that if he were to have looked, it would have been a very bold move. By turning his face away, he suggests that it wasn't his goal to see God, for to see God was to impinge upon God's holiness. By turning his face, he submitted to God's authority. He didn't try to compete with God's glory or to subvert God's sovereignty. He knew that God was not to be fully comprehended. It was his way of saying "wow." It was Moses putting his mind and his body in the right posture for worship.

Rev. Starsky Wilson kicked off this revival by preaching on how we often evaluate the worship of other people. Everyone has a different way of responding to the presence of God. Sometimes, it *does* "take all of that." When I think of how awesome God is and when I get a glimpse of God's glory, I simply *must* respond according to *my* style, *my* sensibilities, and the movements of *my* soul. I owe God my authentic self, just as God created me. I owe God my authentic worship, just as God lays it on my heart. Sometimes, when I think of the goodness of Jesus, it *does take all of that!* When God introduces God's Self to us in worship, it is an opportunity to see our own authenticity, and then to give it back to God in worship.

3. He received an assignment.

After God got his attention, and Moses came into a posture of submission, God told him, "I've seen the afflictions of my people, I've heard their cries, and I've known their suffering. I have come to rescue them." God's people were suffering on every side, and God had a plan for their deliverance. God saw that the situation was so bad that God came down to see about them and to liberate them.

God has a plan for our deliverance. My people, my people, let us not get weary. God has a plan for our escape, and it includes God's personal involvement. Right now, God is looking for agents who are willing to go on assignment and co-labor with God in our deliverance.

God found a willing agent in Moses. Moses was willing to be interrupted and inconvenienced for the call of God. He was willing to worship God, and he had a love for his people. So, God gave him an assignment. In verse 10 it says, "Now, go, I am sending you to Pharaoh to bring my people the Israelites out of Egypt."

It's important that this came last because the assignment would bring pressure, and it would bring fame. Perhaps this is why worship is so dangerous. Not only because it changes who we are, but also because it comes with a responsibility to do some work. "So now, go." You are a real worshipper, so now go. You came here tonight to draw closer to God, so now go. God has arrested your attention; you've seen some strange things, so now go. Worship prepares us to go and do because we've been changed by being in the presence of the Presence so that we can be that presence in the world. Is there anybody who is ready for a new assignment? Did you come here to worship?

Alright, we have worshipped. Now, go and do your work!

LIVE INTO THE CROWN

EPHESIANS 3:14-16 (NRSV)

Preached February 2015, Wake Forest Divinity School, Winston-Salem, NC

I am privileged to serve at Trinity United Church of Christ, where every Black History Month our entire church is transformed for the *MAAFA*: a month-long liturgical odyssey into the African Diaspora through art, music, preaching, drama, dance, and enfleshed history. On first Sunday, we begin on the shores of Africa and in the belly of slave ships; we then make our way to the Caribbean on second Sunday; New Orleans on the third, and end up right on our own block of the South side of the Chi on the fourth Sunday. Naturally, we do Black History Month big. After all, we are "unashamedly Black and unapologetically Christian."

Throughout Black History month, you are likely to see one of our children or teens dressed up as a character from Black History, walking throughout the edifice and teaching people about who they are and what they did. Recently, we were joined in worship by Queen Nanny of the Maroons, a Black woman who fearlessly raided countless plantations in Jamaica, searching for slaves aching for freedom. Queen Nanny of the Maroons was a Black woman who had freed so many slaves that she decided to establish an entire village of free people in the mountains of Jamaica and call it the Maroon Village.

I thought it right and fitting that she has come to be known as Queen Nanny. She was a queen who nurtured her people. She valued the freedom of her people so much that she risked her life for them on an ongoing and continual basis. She was a woman determined to manifest a vision of liberation that not only freed slaves, but also ensured that they remained free. This woman was so persuaded of the value, the beauty and the preciousness of her people that she gave her life for them and their freedom.

Queen Nanny teaches us that you can't crown someone else before you wear your own crown. She was so persuaded of her own value that it was impossible for her not to see the value in her people and vice-versa. You can't love your people without loving yourself. If you do, I would venture to say that you've excluded the most important person from your equation of love because you can't love others when you don't love yourself. You have a skewed sense of love when you're dependent on the love of others in order to love yourself.

Similarly, it seems to me that just as Queen Nanny was clear that she was called to free slaves, Paul was clear that he was called to preach to the Ephesians. While Paul was committed to converting this Gentile church into full-fledged believers and followers of Jesus, Queen Nanny was committed to converting these slaves into free people, righteous rebels, and queens and kings.

She believed that even if the world would call them "slaves," they were more than that. She believed that even if they were relegated to plantations, they were called, by God, into a wide space of freedom at the tops of mountains. She believed that despite the capitalistic foundations of slavery, they were worth more than their bodies and their labor. You couldn't pay *for* these people, and even if you tried, you wouldn't be able to afford them. These people, according to Queen Nanny, were royalty; their feet were waiting to walk on golden streets, their heads awaiting crowns.

Similarly, Paul saw the potential of the Ephesians. He saw them making small movements towards their destiny, and thought it not robbery to, as it says in the text, "fall upon his knees in prayer" on their behalf. Paul saw where the Ephesians were headed and who they could be if they really embraced their freedom in Jesus Christ . . . if they really *believed in* Jesus Christ.

To an outsider looking in, Paul decided that it was worth it to do whatever it took for this community of people to *get it*, and to live into the crown made of supernatural love, supernatural power, supernatural acceptance and affirmation that were already theirs. They just had to live into it.

In preparing today's message, I said to God, "*God, I'm going into a seminary. Why can't I just preach something to help them get through the papers and politics; something to help them endure the stress of field placement and the pressure of what's coming after seminary? Why not a simple message about how to survive seminary?*"

And, as clear as day, God replied to me, "*Because if they get this, they will be able to survive and thrive all the way through seminary and beyond. They will survive the stress of wondering what's next. They will survive the unexpected twists and turns of ministry and life, if they understand that they have been crowned with my unconditional love, my impenetrable protection and my enduring grace. I have crowned them with authority. I have crowned them with victory, and my first call to them is that they live into it.*"

Howard Thurman, great theologian, preacher, philosopher and Morehouse man, famously stated that, "over the heads of her students, Morehouse holds a crown that she challenges them to grow tall enough to wear."

Similarly, here today in this very chapel, God is holding a crown over each of our heads, and God is challenging us, *pushing us* to grow tall enough to wear our crown. So, just how does one live into the crown of authority that is over his or her head? Let's see what the text offers.

1. You must possess spiritual power.

Be aware that there will also be maleficent presences at work against you in this world. Not just challenges, not just hardships, but presences and experiences so powerful that you can't merely get over them. You've got to work through them. You've got to push through them. They will hang themselves over your head. They will make you want to shrink yourself because you might be afraid to go against them. Until you get the courage to face them, you will never live into your crown.

There will be those experiences and spiritual battles that will cause you to question whether or not you are worthy of your crown. According to Paul, we are all vulnerable to the ways of this world and to the ruler of the kingdom of the air (Eph. 2:2). There are all sorts of evil spiritual forces at work in the world, like:

Patriarchy and sexism
Institutionalized racism at all levels of educational and governmental structures
Racial and religious wars
Police brutality and contempt for black and brown lives and
Constant messages that your life doesn't mean as much as others and the real and necessary battle cry—in 2015—that Black lives matter.

You can't tell me that the devil isn't busy. "*For we wrestle not against flesh and blood, but against but against the rulers, against the authorities, against the powers of this dark world and against the spiritual forces of evil in the heavenly realms* (Eph. 6:12)."

Right there in the beginning of the passage, Paul models what such contentious spiritual conditions calls for: "For this reason—because of all you face and all that is set against you—I kneel before God, and I pray."

Paul is suggesting that if you want to live into your crown, you've got to know the power of prayer. You have got to become familiar with the sound of your voice in intimate dialogue with God and the sound of God's voice talking back to you. You have got to humble yourself before your God on a daily basis. Just as you wouldn't leave or return home without your phone, don't leave and don't return home without praying.

You can't live into your crown without spiritual power. You may want to go out on the frontlines and protest with a sign. You may want to head up to Capitol Hill after divinity school to move and shake up some public policies. You may want to go home and teach the men in your life how to be a womanist or a feminist. You may want to respond to the evils of the world in any number of ways. Trust me, all of this is crown work; but you can't do that work without a clear and solid connection to the Source of your strength and the Strength of your life.

2. You need the Holy Spirit dwelling on the inside.

Second, Paul writes that despite all of this, his prayer for the Ephesians is that they would be strengthened with power through the Spirit of God in their inner being. Despite what is happening on the outside, the power that will sustain you is the power from deep within.

What is on the inside of you? By chance, have you let what you see around you on the outside make its way into the inside? Have you let it into your soul? Has your soul been given over to anxiety? Given over to frustration? Given over the sadness at what is going on *outside*?

Don't let what's on the outside keep you from realizing the power that is inside of you. Power. *Dunamis*. A feminine noun etymologically rooted in *dunami*. It means, to be able, to be capable, strong and powerful, moral power or excellence of soul, *power for performing miracles*, inherent power, residing in a thing by virtue of its nature, or of a state of mind.

You have got to get your mind right about who you are. You have to make up your mind that despite what's happening on the outside, despite the history of our people, despite structural evils and institutionalized hatred, *I am a child of God. My people are children of God.* We are infinitely loved and more than able to overcome. We are more than able to triumph because of the spiritual power within!

What's the power for? It is so that Christ may dwell in your hearts through faith.

If your Christ constantly judges you, tells you that you are wrong, tells you that you're not good enough, tells you that your suffering is more meaningful than your joy, then you're certainly following a colonized Christ. You have learned that from another colonized Christian, and you accepted it to your own demise.

The Christ I'm talking about is the Christ that will dwell in your heart and comfort you with his compassion, ease the pressure you're under with his presence and tell you, "I got you" when you're afraid. The Christ I'm talking about is never short of an affirming word and will never place more on you than you can bear. The Christ I'm talking about is the Christ that will move you to service and liberation work when you realize that his cross wasn't only "just for you," but for the entire world to know the love of this Jesus.

> Do you know that you're loved?
> Do you know that Jesus loves you?
> I'm sure that Jesus is thankful that you've affirmed the call on your life, but do you know that Jesus LOVES YOU,
> just as you are, for who you are?

This is a big love. An unconditional love. A love that accepts and affirms you, right here today. And if you get rooted and established in this love, it will change the way you walk in this world. It will change the way you do life. It will have you walking taller so that you can *stretch* your way into your crown. "I pray that you, being rooted and established in love, may have the ability, the power, to grasp, together with all the saints, How . . . wide . . . long . . . high . . . deep is the love of Christ."

> Some of you have overcome some great odds to be here.
> Some of you have been on the verge of losing your minds.
> Some of you have suffered loss.
> Some of you have been laid out on beds of affliction
> Some of you, at one time or another, walked around confused about life and unable to find your direction.

But you have been filled—on the inside—with the power, the presence, and the love of Jesus Christ, so run on, my brother! Run on, my sister! Run on and make room for all of us where you are going!

3. You need to know you are loved, so that you can be filled.

Then, Paul tells them they are beloved. What is the point of knowing this? *So that you may be filled to the measure of all the fullness of God.* When you become full from eating, you either have to stop eating, or your capacity to hold more has to increase. When your glass becomes full of water or tea or whatever, you have to stop filling it or get a bigger glass. And when you become full of this power and this love, you either have to stop receiving the increase, or you must widen yourself, stretch yourself to receive more—live all the way into your crown.

I contend that you will always need more. When God takes you from glory to glory, and you begin to *get it*, I suggest that you will need to *keep* on growing, stretching, and reaching. Don't stunt your own growth by thinking, "I know what I need to know, I've learned everything that I can about who God is and who God has made me to be."

Don't cap your own capacity for God's fullness. Don't doubt God's ability to provide all that you need and more. Don't doubt God's willingness to use your life in new and unforeseen ways. Don't doubt in God's promise to fill you with what you need to do the work. There is more to you than you know.

> There is always more crown to grow into.
> A crown of love
> A crown of courage
> A crown of wisdom
> A crown of patience
> A crown of power
> A crown of selflessness and
> A crown of forgiveness

As you are living into your crown, know this: it will not always be comfortable. It may be heavy and it might even cause you some pain.

Know this, too: everyone won't like your crown. There will be those who don't like seeing you walk with spiritual authority and moral power. There will be those who get offended at the confidence that you exude when you know that you are loved. There will be those who will hate on your crown.

But wear your crown anyway, and wear it well. There's a book, *Crowns: Portraits of Black Women in Church Hats*. It contains the photos and narratives of generations of Black women in in their church hats—their crowns. In this book, Peggy Knox, a 58-year old childcare provider, gives three rules for wearing a crown. The three rules for how to keep a crown on your head and handle the relationship that other people have with your crown are:

1. **Don't let people touch the hat.** "Don't touch my hat," Peggy warns. "The only person who would touch a woman's hat is a person who doesn't wear hats. Admire it from a distance, honey."
2. **Don't let people knock the hat.** "Sometimes people touch it by accident, but that's still no excuse. All that time that you spent fixing it is gone, just like that."
3. **Don't let people hug too close.** "Church people like to hug, but there's a certain way to hug a woman in a hat. You can't get all up on her, grabbing her around the neck. If you do that, you must not be a person who wears a hat. Because if you wear hats, you already know you're not supposed to get that close when you hug. Both people have to tilt their heads way to the side, in the opposite direction, and leave a little space between you."

These 3 rules for not having your church hat (your crown) knocked off are meant humorously, but they can also apply to your spiritual crown. After all that you go through to get into your crown, watch out for anything that will knock it off. Don't let others knock off your crown, including, dysfunctional families, toxic relationships, so-called friends, or a world that would disparage you.

Each day of our lives, the presence of hate, the presence of apathy, the presence of materialism, and the presence of oppression are wide awake and fully active attempting to knock your crown off of your head. If this is accomplished, if we are stopped from living into our crowns, then the principalities, the rulers of the darkness of this world, and spiritual wickedness in high places have achieved the victory they desired. They have silenced and sidelined us. They have made the world a less loving place, a less holy place, a less peaceful place, a less hopeful place, and a less just place.

So be on the lookout for the crown-knocker-offers. Yes, I coined a word, but you know what I mean. As Sister Knox helped us to see, the main way to avoid this is not to let the crown-knocker-offers get too close to you in the first place. Don't let hate get too close to you, lest you become a hateful person. Don't hang out with apathetic folk, because you will find a reason to stay home and not go out and fight. Don't hang out with materialistic folk who have mall ministries and suffer from *affluenza*. Don't hang around folk who oppress other folk because, after awhile, you will no longer raise your voice about the homophobic jokes, the sexist remarks, and the racist rants. Stay away from the crown-knocker-offers! They will diminish your light and cause you to shrink.

Our crowns have been bought and paid for. All we have to do is live into them. We come from a people who were brought over here on ships and worked for more than 400 years as slaves, but we're here today to pay homage to every ancestor who died for the lives we live today.

I know a Man, who on a Good Friday several millennia ago, had a crown placed upon his head. It was a crown of thorns that drew blood and was meant to be a mockery of his royal status. The funny thing about that crown is that to some it was a mockery, but to others, it was a divine manifestation of the love of God.

It was an uncomfortable and humiliating crown. It was a heavy crown. It was a painful crown. But, he wore it until his work was complete. He wore it until our salvation was complete. He lived into it until his calling was complete.

And he bids us today to live into that crown, to stretch into that crown, to grow into that crown that is already sitting atop of your beautiful head.

PART III

LIBERATING WORDS

These sermons are for those who are desperate for a "breakthrough." For those who need God to do something mighty. These sermons are for those who are stuck, those who are broken, those who are fearful, and those who feel powerless.

I have been there.

Many times, the only thing that got me through, besides the grace of God, was the Word of God. During this time, I found myself taking the advice of my seminary homiletics professor, Leonora Tubbs Tisdale, "preach the Word you need to hear." These words would save my life over and over again. On especially long nights, I would get out of my bed, pull out my manuscripts, and preach to myself in the mirror. I got a lot of good preaching practice doing this.

I don't have much to say about these sermons. I believe that they speak for themselves. I dedicate them to the ones who are "yet holding on." May you be strengthened from within until your change comes. I dedicate these to those who are brave enough to go the therapy, join the support group, take the pill, write in the journal, and speak life-giving words to themselves. These are for those who know that God has more for you to do, and are desperately seeking to live into the call. These sermons are for those who won't give up on God, and won't give up on themselves. These sermons are for those who will not stop praying and believing that things will turn around.

WHEN THE WATER CALLS

MATTHEW 14:22-32 (NRSV) AND ISAIAH 43:1-2 (NRSV)

Preached October 2015, Sisterhood Sunday at Christ Missionary Baptist Church, Memphis, TN.

When I was a young lady growing up in Texas, my parents enrolled my siblings and me into a number of summer vacation activities. We went to camps and workshops—all kinds of lessons. This was to keep us busy and engaged while school was out for the summer. The activity that I remember the most was the swimming lessons at the neighborhood pool. Every other day, the three of us would walk to the pool for our lessons with our instructor. I don't remember his name, but let's call him Mike. Mike was a patient swimming instructor, especially with me. My brother has always had natural athletic ability, and so swimming came easy to him. My sister has always been naturally competitive, so even if she didn't like to swim, she would swim, if only to just try her hand at it and to show up her brother and sister. And then, there was me. I brought a host of issues to the pool everyday, including that I always preferred more academic settings and activities to athletic ones. Also, I hated how cold the water was when I first jumped in. Then, of course, I hated getting my hair wet. After all, I am a black woman, and at an early age, I hated that I would have to repeatedly wash the chlorine out of my hair, style it, and then do it all over again just because of swimming lessons. However, my biggest issue with swimming lessons was that I was afraid of the deep water. I could manage on the shallow end, because I mastered wallowing pretty quickly. It wasn't until Mike wanted to introduce me to more advanced swimming methods and styles that I became afraid. Why? Because these could only be done at the opposite end of the pool . . . in deeper water.

Mike was patient with me. He would hold me up as I tried to swim across the pool; but, I could *always* feel when I was crossing over from the shallow side into the deep side. I could always feel the water begin to tug and pull on me, as if it was trying to swallow me. Repeatedly, I would give up trying to cross over to the other side. Finally, Mike got my attention. He told me this: "I am your instructor. I have been trained. I am holding you up until you make it to the other side. You have to trust me and lean into my grip because I will not let you go."

He proved to be a man of his word. It took weeks for me to cross over to the other side because I had to trust in him to help me overcome my fear of the deep water. Yet, slowly but surely, I learned the difference between the feeling of his hands and the feel of the water, and I learned that as long as I kept stroking, neither of these would let me fall. As long as I kept kicking my legs, I would stay afloat. As long as I took quick and deep breaths, I would stay afloat. You can imagine the celebration amongst my siblings, and especially from Mike, when I finally swam from the shallow end to the deep end of the water.

I learned several things from swimming lessons, and from my swim to the deep end.

1. I learned that if I ever wanted to advance and grow up from my mastered skill of wallowing in shallow water, I would have to get the courage to swim to the other side where the water was deeper. The shallow water didn't place a demand on my *courage*, or even on my capabilities.
2. I learned that real brothers and sisters aren't watching you falter to fault you or to taunt you. Rather, like my siblings, they want to see you succeed and they are waiting for the opportunity to celebrate you.

3. I learned that in the hands of a good instructor, you can easily transition from the shallow end to the deep end, but you *must* trust your coach.
4. And, finally, I learned that fear, anxiety, and even unwillingness don't stand a chance against a Black woman who is determined to kick and stroke her way into the deep waters.

And since it is Sisterhood Sunday, and I'm talking about what it means to be "water-walking women," I wonder what this text has to share about crossing over to the other side, from the shallow water to the deep water. What do you do when the deep in God calls to the deep in you? When deep calls unto deep? When the shallow waters are no longer sufficient and when the wallowing becomes offensive to the gifts of God within you? What do you do when you begin to hear the waters calling out to you to come on out here, stretch yourself and walk? What do you do when the waters call?

In today's Gospel text, we see that these disciples are out on some deep waters. They were out on the waters . . . the raging waters . . . the wind-battered waters . . . the wild and whirlwind-like waters.

They were too far from the where they started to turn around, and too close to where they were going to give up out on those waters . . . those vulnerable waters that tossed their boat to and fro, all night long.

But, they'd been on these waters before. You know that back in chapter 8, they'd been in a similar situation. They'd found themselves in the belly of the ocean, caught out on the waters, in the middle of a storm. Chapter 8, verse 24 tells us that a windstorm came and the waters swamped their boat.

The text also tells us that Jesus was on the boat, asleep. Here we have the fundamental difference between these two water storm scenarios: the presence of Jesus. In the first one, Jesus is on the boat. He's asleep, but he's there the entire time. In this second one, Jesus isn't there. You'll remember at the beginning of the story, we see that Jesus was in need of some quiet and alone time, and so he put his disciples on the boat and told them to go to the other side without him.

Again, in one scenario, we see that Jesus is with them *through the storm*. In another, we see that Jesus comes to them *in the midst of the storm*. Despite the variations on his presence and his whereabouts in both scenarios, we see that in neither of them did any disciple die, none drowned, none threw themselves overboard, and none even came down with a case of seasickness. Why? Because regardless of where Jesus was and when he showed up among them physically, he was always there, stabilizing his disciples in the midst of their storms.

We know that these scenarios could have played out very differently. If you think about the storms that you've faced in your life—if you're really honest now that you've come *through* them—you know they *could have been a lot worse* than what they were. There were situations you faced that very well could have taken you out, but because of the presence of Jesus, you are still here, walking on dry land.

> Somebody in here should be dead, paralyzed, or in a mental health institution, but because Jesus was with you,
> You were rescued.
> You were saved.
> The plans of the enemy were interrupted—matter of fact; they were cancelled.

You could have been exposed in your confusion and your sin, but Jesus was present to cover and keep you. You could have drowned in your depression and your anxiety, but Jesus was present to speak to those waves before they consumed you.

Does anyone in the sanctuary have a praise report for what *could have been*, but wasn't because *Jesus was present*? Are you thankful for what didn't happen? Are you thankful for the consequences you didn't have to face and the experience you didn't have because *Jesus was present*?

It gets tricky here because Jesus was present in the second storm; but, Jesus was present in a way that the disciples didn't recognize. They thought he was a ghost. Granted, they'd been on their boat through what was probably a long and sleepless night. And we all know that sleepless nights can be disorienting. Moreover, it was still dark; the text says that it was shortly before the dawning of the sun. Scholars suggest that it might have been between 3 and 6 a.m. So, they weren't just tired, they were surrounded in darkness.

Next, the text says that the disciples were afraid. They thought they were seeing a ghost, when it was really Jesus. This was *the same Jesus* that chose them and commissioned them. This was the same Jesus they'd spent so much time following and getting to know. *The same Jesus* that they'd spent so much time serving and watching. Wouldn't you think that they'd recognize his form and his frame as he walked towards them?

Why would they be afraid at the sight of someone they knew? I believe, again, it wasn't that it was dark. *It wasn't that they were tired. It was that they didn't recognize Jesus, because Jesus was doing something they'd never seen him do before.*

Yes, they had seen him lay his hands on the sick and cure them; they had seen him heal with his word; they had seen him sleep, eat, and travel; they had seen him breathe, and they had seen him do everyday and supernatural God-like things, *but of all the things they'd seen him do, they'd never seen him walk on water before.* They were terrified when Jesus revealed another level of his power and another facet of his identity.

To all of the water-walking women and water-walking men in the sanctuary today, you must be careful when you begin to operate in a new level of your God-given gifting or your divine capacity. You will surprise people. You will make them speechless. You will make some people afraid, even if they are close to you—simply because they are used to seeing you operate on a lower level, when there really is so much more to who you are than what they have seen.

This was the case with Jesus on this stormy night out on the waters. On this fateful night, only one wanted to come closer to a version of Jesus that he'd never seen. Everyone else chose to stay behind in the boat, except for Peter. It's lonely in new waters.

Peter is an interesting figure. We don't have a psychological profile of Peter, but there are a few things that we do know. We know that he was the first disciple that Jesus called, along with his brother Andrew. We know that he denied Jesus three times, but he would go on to confess and testify that Jesus was the Son of God, and it was on his confession that Jesus built his Church. And, we know from this story that he was the only one who was courageous enough to get out of the boat and walk on the water towards Jesus.

We know something else about him. He was a fisherman so we can assume that Peter was used to being out on the waters. What he did for a living required that he be out on the waters, probably at various times of the day and night. Peter knew his way around the waters. He knew the water patterns. He knew when the water might render the greatest catch. He knew these waters. *But, he only knew the waters from inside of a boat.*

After all, he was a fisherman and every fisherman needs a boat. Or, *was* he just a fisherman? Did he really *need* a boat?

In this text, we see that the boat was struggling. It struggled to make headway because, the text says, the calamitous winds were pushing against it. In an ideal situation, the winds would push the boat along . . . but, not tonight. Tonight, the wind was working against the boat. Not only was it unstable, or even worse, it might be moving backwards.

I think Peter had an impulse greater than that of merely a fisherman. He had probably learned a lot and grew a lot from being a fisherman, but like everyone with a greater calling upon their life, Peter was probably beginning to feel like there was more to him than just being a fisherman. Perhaps, he'd been relegating his identity for so long to what he did, he made the common mistake of collapsing what he did and who he was. If Peter could speak, I believe he'd tell many of us today, *"You are not what you do."*

You have to be careful when you wrap up your entire identity and purpose and self-worth in what you do, because there is a difference. For example, I preach. That's what I do.

But, I identify as a child of God with a hunger for the world to know Jesus. That's who I am. I teach. That's what I do. But, I identify as a woman who believes in the liberation of women, that's who I am.

Understanding this is important for two reasons. First, God loves me for who I am, not for what I do. If God loved me for what I did, I'd have to keep doing it for God to continue loving me.

Second, who I am is ultimately a reflection of God, which means that there is no limit to what I can do. I can do all things!

If you want to be a water-walking woman, perhaps you need to break out of the box of what you do, and focus more on who you are. Because this is what Peter did. The only thing standing between Peter and the water that was calling him was the boat. The boat symbolized the box of "what I do" for Peter. I imagine it was a very interesting place to be in that moment. I bet Peter wondered, "who would I be and what could I accomplish if I finally got out of this boat?"

Indeed, Peter is an interesting figure in this story. Furthermore, the boat is also interesting.

Peter might've known the waters, but he knew the boat even better. He had always been in the boat. After all, he was a fisherman, and the boat was his domain. It was safe and it was secure. It gave him a sense of power; he knew how to steer it. He knew how to control it. He knew what it was purposed to do. It was familiar, therefore it also gave him a false sense of security. As long as Peter was in the boat, Peter did the same thing, performed the same tasks, and lived to the same capacity every day. As long as he was in it, Peter was almost stunting his own growth. The boat didn't challenge him. It didn't stretch him. The boat was comfortable to him; but, my brothers and sisters, the paradox is that it was also confining.

I would think that if you want to be a water-walking woman, you have got to be acutely aware of the thin line between comfort and confinement. In either case, a water-walking woman must recognize when it's time to get out of the boat. You've got to recognize when the place where you have been is no longer sufficient for who God is calling you to be. You've got to recognize when you can't stay where you've been because it's time to go deeper, to be stretched wider. You've got to recognize when the water is calling you.

How do you know that the water is calling? Peter might suggest a couple of ways. First, you feel frustrated all the time. You feel confined and underutilized. You're ready for a new experience. Second, you have exhausted your possibilities and capabilities in one place, and you just feel like it's time to move on. Next, you continue to have the same experiences, and it is as if you're going in circles. Peter had been here before, almost shipwrecked on a raging sea. Based on that experience, he knew that with Jesus present, everything would be alright. There should be some experiences that you only need to have one time in order to get the lesson. Finally, the company you keep is no longer in agreement with what the Spirit is telling you. While the disciples were crying out in fear, Peter was thinking, "I want to try something different."

But, before he could get out of the boat, three things needed to happen. First, he needed to confirm that it was really Jesus. Peter realized that he was risking his life. And in such a situation, you need a reason that is worth taking the risk. For Peter, it wasn't about merely walking on the water. "Lord, if it is *you*," said Peter. Not, "Lord, if it is more money, prestige, notoriety, and popularity." Not, "if it is more exposure, or more accolades for me." Your motive for stepping out of your boat *must* only be to get to Jesus. "If it is *you*."

"If *you* are also on the water."
"If *you* meet me out on the deep."

When the waters call, they are not calling you to consume you. They are calling to draw you closer to Christ. That's what all of this is about: getting closer to Jesus. It's about becoming more like Jesus. When the water calls, and your motive for walking out on the water is right, you can guarantee that Jesus is also out on the waters. Jesus, too, wants a closer walk with you. In fact, that's what he wants most.

Next, Peter prayed a bold prayer. Verse 28 says, "Tell me to come to you on the water." Wow! That's a bold prayer. A Peter-like prayer. It suggests that it's time to stop praying puny prayers. Powerless prayers. It's time to stop praying the prayers you heard someone else pray or the prayers you've prayed your whole life. When the water calls, your default prayers won't do. Your self-loathing, sorry prayers have got to go. Moreover, it suggests that you can't only pray when you feel like it. A bold prayer life is developed over time.

"God, umm . . . hi, it's me . . . I'm not sure if you hear me . . ." must eventually turn into "God of the Universe, God of the waters, I come to Your throne boldly, confident in Your power to keep me, as I move closer to You." Water-walking women are women who *know* that the *fervent* and effectual prayers of the righteous availeth much—and they excite the heart of God. They pray that they will be available to God, that they are bold enough to take risks, and that they will always depend on God. They pray prayers of activation. Then their prayers are followed by action. These are the prayers of water-walking women.

Finally, Peter waited for a word of instruction. Often, we want to jump into things, and do unfathomable things without consulting God. Perhaps your frustration and your agitation in the boat has gotten so bad, that if you don't bust a move NOW, you will certainly lose your mind, never mind the fact that you haven't asked God for permission, and you definitely haven't heard God say, "come."

Let me insert here that I get so tired of all of these people popping up talking about, "I'm going to be a preacher. I can preach." They think that just because they can whoop and make an audience shout, that they've been given divine license to preach this Gospel. But, they can't recall an experience of being *called*. They came up with some brilliant idea, some conceited impulse for their own fame, coming up behind the sacred desk, playing with peoples' lives, playing with their minds and their salvation, and have never heard God say "come" out on these waters! You've got to know when you are being called by the water—and the God of the water—and when you're being called by your ego.

Peter was able to confirm that it was Jesus he had heard, and he lifted a mighty prayer. Then, out of the dark and through the wind and the waves, he heard the familiar voice of Jesus say, "come." I believe Peter's faith excited Jesus. I think this is the kind of faith that makes Jesus say bold things to us, like "Come."

We know what happened when Jesus said come. Peter went, without hesitation and trepidation. With confidence in himself and with confidence in Jesus, the text says that Peter got down out of the boat, walked on the water and came toward Jesus. One of the greatest disservices that we can do to Peter is to overlook this part of the story. We all know he started to sink, but why do we skip over the fact that he *did walk on the water*, for a few short steps? With precise focus on Jesus and full of confidence in the call of the water, he got out of the boat. He *tried*! He didn't know what would happen if he got out of the boat, but he did know what would happen if he stayed in the boat. He'd keep on doing the same thing that he'd always done. But, he didn't stay. He got out of the boat. He attempted to water-walk. Peter gave it a try. If you want to walk on water, you've got to try something that you've never done before.

He actually walked on water, until he didn't anymore. I don't want to stay here longer than to say that just as much as water-walking is possible, it's also possible to sink. It's also possible to fail. You have to weigh the possibilities. Is it worth more to you to try and possibly succeed? Or is it worth more to you to not try and fail, for not trying? What is your perspective on the possibilities? Are you willing to take this risk?

In the event that you start to sink, for whatever reason, Peter gives a clue as to what to do. He asked for help. "Lord, save me." He asked for help. I know that we like to do it all on our own; we like to act like we're in control and like we've got it all together. We like to put on our best outfits and our highest heels, even if we're walking on water, and put forth the appearance that we don't need help. But, oh, every now and then, you will need to ask for help to do something new and bold.

Jesus was out on the water, and if you think that Jesus' water-walking was the God-side of him showing, imagine the power that was harnessed when he heard Peter cry out, "Lord, save me."

You'll remember that when he first encountered his disciples in the boat, being tossed on the waters by the winds, the first thing he said was, "It is I." Research shows that at the etymological root of this word, this is a Greek clause that can literally be translated, "I am." This is the literal translation of the Tetragrammaton, the unspeakable four-letter name of the God we serve, YHWH. In other words, Jesus was not only saying, "I'm here, don't be afraid," he was also saying "*I AM and I am with you.*"

Don't you just love it when God shows up in all of God's power and all of God's ability and all of God's power, presence, and Godness right when you need it the most?

I AM was there to respond the cry of Peter. Immediately, Jesus stretched out his hand and caught Peter. Jesus reached out his hand, and Peter was saved by the hand of *I AM* . . .

the one who holds the winds in his hands . . .
the same hands that were laid on the sick . . .
the same hands that brought sight to the blind . . .
the same hands that broke bread for the multitudes.

These were the same hands that caught Peter as he was sinking.

I wonder if there's anyone in the sanctuary that knows about the hands of the great I AM?

We are in the hands of that *I AM*.
We are kept by the hands of *I AM*.
We are covered by the hands of *I AM*.
We are rescued by the hands of *I AM*!

Does anyone know about the hands of *I AM*?
Someone knows that these hands will provide for you.
Someone knows these hands will open doors for you.
Someone knows that these hands will clear paths for you.
Someone knows these hands can pick you up and clean you up.
And, someone knows These hands can turn you around, and place your feet on a solid ground.

These hands of the Great *I AM*!

We can be water-walking women, because we are in the hands of the Great I AM.

GO GET YOUR JOY

PSALM 126:1-6, EMPHASIS 5-6 (NRSV)

Preached August 2013, Trinity UCC, Chicago, IL

> Joyful, joyful, we adore Thee, God of glory, Lord of love;
> Hearts unfold like flowers before Thee, opening to (or Hail Thee as) the sun above.
> Melt the clouds of sin and sadness; drive the dark of doubt away;
> Giver of immortal gladness, fill us with the light of day!

The words of this poem, *Joyful, Joyful, We Adore Thee*, were penned by Henry Van Dyke, an early twentieth-century clergyman, known for his intellectual fervor and remarkable oratory and narrative skills. In 1907, Van Dyke was on sabbatical and became so inspired by the Berkshire Mountains in New England that he wrote this poem. In 1911, Van Dyke published the text and said this about it: "These verses are simple expressions of common Christian feelings and desires in this present time . . . Therefore this is a hymn of trust and joy and hope."

My brothers and sisters, while I find the words of this poem beautiful in their eloquence and thoughtful in their typological reflection, I struggle with Van Dyke's explanation of the words. To suggest that this is hymn for those "who know the thought of the age" and, who are worried about "any truth of science" destroying religion, or "revolutions on earth overthrowing the kingdom of heaven," is to say that he didn't intend this to be a hymn for all people, most specifically the folk and the people. Y'all know the folk and the people. Those whose lives were much simpler, and still more complex, and whose minds were preoccupied with living from day to day with a sense of safety and dignity. I mean, I'm sure that 1907 was similar to today in that not everyone was able to take a break from their jobs to go sojourn in the mountains of New England.

Moreover, I struggle with the idea that this is a song about "common Christian feelings." I'd like to have a talk with the writer of this poem, and I'd like to ask him, Mr. Van Dyke, have you ever had a bad day? Have you ever been disappointed in something or in someone? Have you ever been sad, and despite your best efforts to shake it, it didn't go away?

I'm sure we'd have some interesting conversations. I'm sure that we'd end up on some common ground because, certainly, I, too, believe that trust, joy, and hope are *ideal* Christian feelings, but are they common? It seems to me that I've spent many days waiting for my trust in God to be reinvigorated, for my hope to be divinely stirred within me, and for joy to come beaming from my soul like a light from a lighthouse on a dark night out on a raging sea.

I have memories, some distant and some more recent that I'd like to admit, of crying myself to sleep at night and not wanting to get up in the morning. I can recall the feeling of despair weighing so heavily on me that I felt as if my heart was at my feet, and I was almost immobilized. I know what it feels like to feel lost, with no sense of direction and no readily available compass. I know what it feels like to pray to God for a moment of relief from the pain and disappointment and regret within, and feel like God wasn't responding fast enough. Is there anybody in here with me, that can say that you know how it feels to be on the verge of tears for no apparent reason, and feeling as if the very slightest agitation will cause the floodgates to swing open wide?

Is there anybody in here who has felt as if you were on the verge of losing it, but you just couldn't say anything because you were worried that you'd be called crazy, or at least looked upon like you were crazy? Is there anybody in here with me that knows how it feels to be *desperate for joy?*

Well, we are not alone. In fact, there is a mighty nation in the word of God that was familiar with these feelings and experiences of despair and displacement. They struggled with God and they struggled to do right by God, and before they knew it, they were in exile, banished from the home that God had given them and insecure about their future. We read all about their exile in several books of the Hebrew Bible, such as 2 Kings, Ezra, Jeremiah, and hear their song of lament in Psalm 137:

> *By the rivers of Babylon we sat and wept*
> *when we remembered Zion.*
> *There on the poplars*
> *we hung our harps,*
> *for there our captors asked us for songs,*
> *our tormentors demanded songs of joy;*
> *they said, "Sing us one of the songs of Zion!"*
> *How can we sing the songs of the Lord*
> *while in a foreign land?*

So, we know this is a people who can identify with the experience of the blues:

Anxiety.
Bad moods.
Melancholy.
Depression.

But, in Psalm, we see that this was also a people who knew what it meant to be delivered from the dumps, and what it felt like to beat the blues. It is there in the text. They have gone from hanging up their harps, and shutting down their song to opening their mouths with laughter and shouts of joy, because of what God has done for them.

We know that God is in the business of turning things around. God delights in intervening on our behalf, even when it seems as if God is taking God's sweet time doing it. In times of despair, it's often so perplexing and disorienting that we give up the possibility that God can move our hearts and restore our joy. This is when the problem sets in. When we give up on God, we give up on ourselves. When we give up on ourselves, we resign ourselves to our sad lots in life. You all know all of the dead-end and deadly places that self-resignation can take us to.

While we see here in the text that God doesn't leave us in despair, the reality is that sometimes we leave ourselves there. We stop choosing hope. We stop fighting back. We stop getting up and putting one foot in front of the other.

I don't know what your story is. It could be a devastating word from a doctor,
    a disappointed dream,
    an unanticipated divorce,
    rejection from the clique or college of your choice,
    domestic violence,
    the loss of a loved one,
    or maybe there's no clear reason at all that you can put your finger on.
    You can't name the source of the pain.

Or, maybe, it's the issues that we all share:
    our children under siege,
    our rights being stripped away from us and more laws legalizing our demise, schools being shut down,
    old debt, new debt, just all of the debt,
    unease in our neighborhoods and in our homes,
    degrading images that harm our boys and our girls and constant stress!

No matter what the reason, you're stuck with the emotional and mental repercussions, and for *some reason*, you just can't shake it. Just as I told you that I'm acquainted with the blues, I can also tell you that I'm acquainted with that one critical moment when you have to *decide*—just like the people in the text—that *I'm done with the blues.*

Sometimes, when it seems as if joy just isn't running to you, you've got to get up and go get it. God has already promised that the final word is victory. God has already turned the page by securing our joy in Christ. So, perhaps it's time for some of us to wake up, pull ourselves up off our beds, place our feet on the floor, and get moving. Perhaps it's time to stop thinking that things can't change, you can't do better, and you can't have joy. As we look into these two verses, God gives us a few guidelines for how to go and get our joy.

1. Let your tears fall

"Restore our fortunes, O Lord, like the watercourses in the Negev. May those who sow in tears reap with shouts of joy." Here, while the Psalmist is grateful for what God has already done, the Psalmist is asking God to complete the work. *Now, that we're back here, send us some water, some rain, some nourishment, a sign of your favor among us.* The Negev is an area in the far south of Palestine, known for its arid climate and desert-like conditions. But, periodically, the Negev would experience seasons of downpour that would come and nourish the land.

I don't think that it's by coincidence that the writer asks for a downpour of rain just before he raises the fact that when your soul is weary and your spirit is broken, a natural response is to weep. To cry. To let it all out.

It's a shame that there are erroneous gender norms and socialization tactics that arise around the act of crying. Crying, somehow or another, has become a feminized activity, something that only women do—or *should* do. And only little girls at that, because apparently, "big girls don't cry." Crying, unfortunately, is often taken as a sign of weakness in women and in men. It is supposedly reserved for the faint of heart and for those who are prone to drama.

But, we know differently. Many of us in this room tonight can attest to a moment in which we sat down for a good cry, one much like the one Toni Morrison described in the book *Sula*: "loud and long—but it had no bottom and it had no top, just circles and circles of sorrow." And many of us know that somehow once we were "all cried out," we felt lighter, we felt calmer, and we felt a little less discombobulated. Moreover, God sees our tears differently. God sees crying as an exercise of the human soul—an expression of our very real and legitimate anguish and pain. Psalm 56: 8 tells us that our tears are so valuable to God, that God saves them all in a bottle.

The writer affirms that our tears are not in vain. For those of us who have "sown in tears," there is a promise of songs of joy. Interestingly, in the Word, there seems to be an inextricable dance between weeping and joy. As if you can't have one without the other. In multiple places, they are linked together.

Psalm 30:5 says that, "weeping may endure for a night, but joy comes in the morning." Psalm 30:11 testifies that God will turn your mourning into dancing! And, in Psalm 126, God is getting a message through, that *if you want to get through to joy, sometimes you will have to cry, and a good cry will do your spirit a lot of good.*

2. Stop suffering in silence

The next suggestion in the text is that perhaps we have to create a new reality with our words. The text speaks of "songs of joy" and "shouts of joy." In other words, we have to break our own silence. Many of us suffer and never say a word about it. We clam up; we pretend like everything is okay, never reaching out for prayer of guidance or assistance of any kind. We act as if not talking about it will make it go away.

Recently, we had come to the end of our monthly pastoral staff team meeting. We were closing in prayer, and lifting up our prayer requests. I had been going through a lot in my personal life, and I decided to break my silence and ask for prayer. I confessed that I was struggling with my mental and emotional health, and that I was beginning to feel like I had too much going on at once. My teammates laid their hands on me, and covered me in prayer. They called my name before the Lord and asked for my heart to be strengthened.

The morning after, I heard the Spirit of God say, "now that you've broken your silence, you've got to change your confession." Gone were the days when I could just complain about my situation. I began to change how I spoke about my life and the situations that I was facing, and began to feel my attitude changing for the better. Did the situation change? Not as fast I would have liked. But, *I* was changing. This is why the writer tells us that *songs* of joy are good for evoking the *spirit* the joy.

Not songs of happiness or songs of contentment, but songs of joy! Songs of joy are not based on our circumstances, but *on the faithfulness of our God*. This type of joy is what we feel when God is working a change in us, though God may not change our circumstances. Joy is the choice we make to get up in the morning and face the day with boldness because of our God.

My brother, my sister, you must break your own silence! Speak up for yourself. Speak over yourself. Change your confession. "Encourage yourself, in the Lord."

3. Get Up

The final suggestion in the text is that when we are seeking renewed joy, sometimes we have to get up and go get it. "Those who go out weeping, bearing the seeds for sowing, shall come home with shouts of joy, carrying their sheaves."

Three days after the acquittal of Trayvon Martin's murderer, a small number of young adults began to stream into the office of Florida's Republican State Governor, Rick Scott. Their plan was simple: to stage a sit-in to protest of the intrinsic racism of Florida state law, specifically of the Stand Your Ground provision. The group formed shortly after Trayvon's death. They sat in at the Governor's Office for four weeks, gaining small victories along the way. They did get the attention of the governor, who agreed to listen to them, and did so for an hour. He did not call a special session evaluating the law, but he *listened* to them. According to an article in the New York Times, they've attracted the attention and support of Harry Belafonte, and Talib Kweli. Florida House Speaker Will Weatherford announced that he would ask a House subcommittee to conduct a hearing this fall on Stand Your Ground, another small victory.

Their story illustrates a final suggestion that's in the text. Sometimes, you have to get up from the situation that's draining the life out of you. In the context of this scripture, the writer is suggesting that in times of drought, it was a major risk to get up and sow seed. It was such a risk that it induced anxiety and could have even brought one to weep. Would God actually send the rain? Would this be a waste of seed, a waste of energy, a waste of money, a waste of time, a waste of hope?

I want to let you know that to one who is desperate for joy, just the possibility that God *could* send the rain could make the difference between your defeat and your joy. When you get tired enough of the pain and when you've cried enough tears, this text suggests that it might be time to pick yourself up and start sowing some seeds. Sowing some seeds of *hope* because there's *a chance* that God could send some rain. Hope that God can turn something around. Hope that, *although I don't know how this new thing will end up, it will sho' nuff be better than what I got going on right now!*

> And, so if you want to get your joy, get up.
>> Does a job have you down? Get up.
>> Stuck in a bad relationship? Get up.
>> Tired of making the same mistake? Get up!
>> Tired of going in circles? Get up!
>> Tired of wasting time when you could be pursuing purpose? Get up!
>> Tired of saying, "Yes" to the wrong people? Get up!
>> Tired of our babies dying in the streets? Get up!
>> Tired of our babies being miseducated and uneducated? Get up!
>> Tired of enduring domestic violence. Get up.
>> Tired of saying no to God? Get up!

Get up, and go get your joy!
No one can stop you, but you.
It's yours.
> You deserve it.
> It's not too late.
> It's possible.
> It's ordained.

So, go get your joy!

THE ANATOMY OF A TESTIMONY

PSALM 107:2-9 (NRSV)

Preached August 2012, Grace United Church of Christ, Milwaukee, WI

A testimony is not just a bunch of words. It is more than a story, more than a memory. It is a collection of words that represent a lived experience. It points to a God who is alive and real and present and awesome. If you have experienced the redemption of the Lord, this psalm compels you to tell someone something about it. Say something good about God. Tell someone the story of what God has done for you.

How do you know that you have a testimony? What are you supposed to say when giving a testimony? This psalm points us in the direction of some answers to these questions.

1. Our testimonies bear witness to life's resistance and our remorse.

Everybody goes through hardship. Trouble is a part of life. Trouble is an existential reality to the human experience, and to some, trouble is detrimental. It causes a loss of faith and confidence in God. Trouble can be so bad that it causes one to just give up and give out.

In life, we experience a lot of resistance. Resistance is when you try to move forward, but life is pushing at you from the opposite direction. You try to climb up but the gravity of life's circumstances weighs too heavily on your back and pulls you down. It seems as if progress is not progressing. This is resistance.

But, to the one who holds on through trouble, through hell, through resistance, this is the beginning of a testimony. *Resistance is the catalyst for change for the one who holds on.* A testimony may begin with trouble—with resistance. And, this text tells us something critical because it is *the way we respond to resistance that leads to testimony.* Verse 6 says, "Then they cried to the Lord in their trouble." This is remorse, or crying out to the Lord. I have heard some pretty intense crying in my life, in and outside the church house. I have also done a lot of crying of my own. It seems that at several major junctures in my life, my eyes were full of tears. Tears born of questions, tears born of fears, tears born of fatigue. It is as if crying to God was a ritual that occurred just before God turned something around in my life.

I have learned something very significant about crying out to God, something very powerful about tears. Your cry to God sends out a signal to God that "I'm in need! I've reached my limit and I need your help!" Our tears to God signify, *I need YOU to come in and rescue me from these drowning waters, to save me from these walls that are closing in all around me.*

Crying is also a sign of remorse over mistakes that we've made, impulses that we acted on, negligence in our relationship with God, sadness at how things have turned out, or outrage over that which we appear unable to stop, such as the regular hunting and gunning down of our sons and daughters. Crying is one of the most human, humane, and humbling activities of the human spirit. A cry to God is an "SOS," that comes from that place within that knows when we're nearing desperation and despair.

It is what the people did in this psalm. Verse 6 lets us know that they cried out to God. They looked out at their realities, their resistance, and expressed remorse over how far they'd gotten off of the path. They looked around and no longer saw that land of flowing milk and honey in their line of vision. Instead, there was nothing but desert, nothing but desolation. What was once lush and bright had become destitute and dark. What's worse is that they could find NO WAY OUT.

Do you know what it feels like to have your back against a wall? To feel immobilized by what's going on in your life? To feel like there's nowhere to go? To feel like there is no other option but to remain in that lonely corner, in that isolated cell, in that dry desert?

Well, God has sent me here to prescribe a good cry to you. A good holla. A good shout. You may want to speak honestly to God, and tell God, "Lord, help me! I don't know what I'm going to do if you don't step in and get me from this place!" Express some remorse to God, like the people of God did in verse 6. Cry to the Lord. Release tears. Release rage. Let God know what's troubling you.

Do you know what happens when we hold in pain, rage, frustration, and anger? It eats us up from the inside and then eats us up outside. It impacts us emotionally, and we want to stop being angry, sad, and outraged, but we can't because we're holding everything inside. We want to forgive, move on, and love again, but we can't because we're holding on to old stuff. This affects our heart rate, our blood pressure, our breathing, our sleep, our hair growth, and our weight. In other words, it has a holistic impact on our entire beings. Holding on to past hurts, hurts us and usually makes us hurt others. That's why you hear the axiom, "Hurt people hurt people." I know that it sounds cliché, but it is certainly true.

Do you think that you can handle this by yourself? Do you think that this battle is yours to fight? Well, as a messenger of God, I want to inform you that you can't. Your arms aren't long or strong enough to battle this on your own. You need to cry out to God, and when you do, open your eyes, and lift them up because you are on your way to a testimony.

So, you have life's resistance and your remorse. This is the beginning of the formation of a testimony, but, it's not the whole story. There's more to a testimony than resistance and remorse.

2. A testimony also includes God's response and restoration.

What I love about this passage is that it bears witness to a God who is moved by the cries of God's people. Immediately after they cried out, it says, "and God delivered them from their distress."

I don't know about you, but I hate the feeling of being ignored. I hate the feeling that I get when I cry out, and it seems as if no one is listening or responding to my cry. I hate the young African-American blood that cries out from the streets of Chicago, seemingly unheard and ignored. What would happen if we heard that blood? What would happen if we heard the silent cry of every youth who is too scared to cry out against the violence in their communities?

We don't know how long the people in the text cried out. We don't know how many tears they shed or how much energy they exerted before God heard and delivered them. We don't know if it took days, months, or years for them to get their answer. No, my brothers and sisters, we don't know that; but we do know THIS: they cried and God heard. They cried until they were delivered, and their persistent cries moved God's heart to respond.

Isaiah 59:1 says, "Surely the arm of the LORD is not too short to save, nor is God's ear too dull to hear." God also tells us in 2 Chronicles 7:14, "If my people, who are called by my name, will humble themselves and pray and seek my face and turn from their wicked ways, then will I hear from heaven and will forgive their sin and will heal their land."

I know it's been a long time for some of you. It seems as if you've cried many tears and paced your floor many nights. It seems as if you have faced so many losses and so few victories. *But, a testimony ain't a testimony until you get to the part where God steps in.*

You may be on your way to your testimony now. Maybe you haven't gotten to the part where God steps in and turns your situation around. I want to encourage you. Not only is it here in the Word that our God is a hearing, seeing, and delivering God, but you are probably sitting next to someone who can tell you from his or her own life, and with his or her own lips, that God can and God will step in, just in the nick of time.

I'm wondering if there's anyone in here with a testimony that God's perfect timing will just blow your mind?

    Just when you thought you were about to lose heart and lose faith,

    just when you thought you were going to give up,

and just when you thought, "this is unbearable," the Lord stepped in!

It was *right then* that the Lord stepped in, delivered you, healed you, heard you, and quieted your mind! God restored to you that which you'd thought you'd lost forever. There was so much that was wrong before God's intervention, but when God stepped in, everything was all right.

Does anybody know that God responds and restores? Is that your testimony?

> You remember that time when . . .
> You recall that one year when . . .
> You know that one day when . . .
> You remember that hour when?

Well, if you remember, you ought to say something about it! This leads to the final point in the anatomy of a testimony.

3. The people respond with telling and rejoicing!

A testimony is not a testimony until you tell it! Testimonies can leave us in tears, but they are tears of joy. These are tears of release, tears of affirmation—tears of a good kind. They are part of the anatomy of a testimony. A testimony is an opportunity to retell what God has done for us. They remind us, renew us, and re-energize us with joy!

Testimonies are even more powerful than that, because testimonies about what God has done for *you* can encourage someone who is waiting for their breakthrough to hold on. Somebody would get their healing if you would just tell your testimony in joy. Yes, God sees your testimony as remembrance and perhaps remorse on your part. But God also needs you to proclaim your testimony, because someone is trying to hold on long enough to get through to the point of proclaiming *their* testimony.

Your testimony can encourage a child who thinks they won't make it out of their neighborhood and into college.

Your testimony can help some senior citizen who is deciding between food and medicine, to lift up their bowed down head.

Your testimony can bring a measure of comfort to some parent whose child has been maliciously gunned down.

Your testimony may give someone hope of an outcome similar to yours. Outcomes may vary, but what is guaranteed is that their hope will be restored, and we know that just a little bit of hope can make all the difference.

> A little bit of hope can save a child from dropping out of school.
> A little bit of hope can stop an adult from hurting a child.
> A little bit of hope can keep marchers marching and picketers on the picket lines.
> A little bit of hope can keep dreamers believing.
> A little bit of hope can give you time to come up with the right idea to change your situation.
> A little bit of hope can help someone hold on long enough to get to their testimony!

So, your testimony is not solely about you! First, it's about what God did, not what you did. Then, it's about some fellow soul who is struggling, battling, tossing and turning trying to get to through to his or her own testimony. Then, it's about your release and your gratitude to God.

That said, please take your turn and tell your story. Stand up and be a witness. Stand up, walk up, and speak up every chance you get. Tell your testimony and rejoice in God's deliverance. Testify. Testify. Testify!

Post it on Facebook, tweet it on Twitter.

> The Lord kept you,
>   forgave you,
>   lifted you,
>   and saved you!

> The Lord dried your tears,
>   lifted your head,

redeemed your children,
renewed your mind,
gave you purpose,
brought you justice,
gave you peace,
birthed in you a dream,
and secured your future!

You've got a reason to rejoice. Testify!

IT'S TIME TO GET EXCITED!

2 CHRONICLES 20:1-12 (NSRV)

Preached April 2013, Trinity UCC, Chicago, IL.

My brothers and my sisters, before I go any further with this word, I'm sure that there may be one or more of you that may be thinking:

"It's Time to Get Excited?" That's a rather interesting thought, preacher, considering the week that we have had. This week has been one for the books. Have you been under a rock, standing here talking about "it's time to get excited?"

Do you not remember what happened less than a week ago, when three innocent people were killed and more than 180 others injured when two explosives detonated at the finish line of the Boston Marathon? Do you not remember that another explosion occurred in a town called West, Texas, killing at least 15 people and injuring close to 200? Meanwhile, our own neighborhoods and streets right here in Chicago were flooded by the waters of torrential rains, threatening our lives in even more ways than they already are?

Yes, I do remember, and I remember several other events that have recently taken place, one involving a U.S. plane dropping a lethal explosive and killing approximately 30 people at an Afghan wedding. I remember the Saudi Arabian man who was nationally accused of committing this act because of what he looked like, not because there was any substantial evidence that connected him to the crime. Yes, I agree. This week has been one to remember for the devastation and the pain, for the sadness and the tears, and for those whose lives were taken.

It has also been a week to remember the first responders who ran towards that blast on Monday, when they could have ran away from it. That made me recall that Jesus himself said, "No greater love has anyone than this, that they would lay down their lives for a friend." It was a week to remember for the way communities banded together to help one another, and for the interfaith prayer service that took place in Boston.

But, most importantly, it was a week to remember the God who orchestrates all of the circumstances of our lives, no matter how grave, how desperate, and how depraved. In fact, I'm thankful that as bad as this was, we've seen worse and we've come through worse because we serve a God who promised in Isaiah 43:2: "When you pass through the waters, I will be with you; and when you pass through the rivers, they will not sweep over you. When you walk through the fire, you will not be burned; the flames will not set you ablaze."

Yes, this promise is one that we, as Black Americans, know very well *from experience*. In fact, *we* have a song that we sing that recalls how faithful our God has been to us and that God has been our help in times past. This song is James Weldon Johnson's "Lift Ev'ry Voice and Sing," and in this song, we beautifully and boldly proclaim that:

> *We have come, over a way that with tears has been watered*
> *We have come, treading out path through the blood of the slaughtered.*

And through it all, it was the:

> *GOD of our weary years, GOD of our silent tears,*
> *Thou Who has brought us thus far on the way*
> *Thou Who hast by Thy might, led us into the light*
> *Keep us forever in the path we pray."*

This is why I am excited. This is why I boldly proclaim it is time for all of us to get excited. Because despite recent activities, we have a God that counts it not robbery to get involved in the circumstances of our lives, and to get down in the "nitty gritty," the not-so-pretty stuff that we go through. When God gets involved, God always does something amazing and leaves us better off than we were before God showed up.

We're all waiting to see what good could possibly come out of the events of this week, and if we're all really honest, we've all seen God show up in some way, shape, or form sometime in the past. We're not the only ones. King Jehoshaphat has a testimony or two about how good God is, and that all you have to do is wait on God to step in and amaze you. He is in our text for today, and he is being pursued. The people he serves are being pursued. The land that they inherited from God is being pursued.

The text says that he was afraid. Of course he was afraid. We can imagine what he was afraid of: out of nowhere, three nations were coming to make war against him. But, he did three critical things to turn his fear into excitement.

1. He was surprised by the attack, but he was not dismayed.

Jehoshaphat hadn't so much as raised a finger against any of these nations, and here they come, starting trouble. In fact, not only had he not done anything wrong towards them, chapter 17 tells us that from the very beginning of his reign, God had been with King Jehoshaphat because he sought to please God and to keep God's commandments. If you read from chapter 17 and beyond, you'll read that "King J" was different from just about every king before him because he was determined to put God back in the center of Judah, back in the middle of the society, and back into the hearts of the people.

He made reform after reform, including fortifying the city against outside influences and dispatching throughout all of the land teachers to teach God's law and Levites to conduct worship. He did so much for God that the text calls him "courageous in the ways of the Lord." Yet despite all of this, here he was on the brink of what would *surely* be a fatal attack.

Have you ever tried so hard to do things right and you still met opposition? It seemed as if you had done everything you knew to do, and still you were faced with resistance. Students, have you ever studied really hard and still didn't make the grade? Have you ever worked hard on the relationship, and it still didn't work out? Have you ever sought the Lord for an answer or a touch, and still felt that God was distant?

Jehoshaphat knows a little something about this too. You might be like Jehoshaphat, or you might not be. This may not be your story. Perhaps you've dropped the ball quite a few times; perhaps you *haven't* given it your all, whatever that is, and now you're in a tight situation of your own creation. Perhaps you've messed things up so badly that if God doesn't step in quick, fast and in a hurry, you don't know how you will make it through.

What we see here is that regardless of our story, we all have a moment in time when we simply need God to step in, an "*I need You now*" moment. In the words of Smokie Norful, "not another second, another minute, or hour of another day. I need you right away!"

> It doesn't matter who you are or who you aren't.
> It doesn't matter who your mama or your daddy is.
> It doesn't matter what your position is.
> It doesn't matter what you've done.
> It doesn't matter how hard you've worked.
> It doesn't matter where you've gone to school.
> It just doesn't matter.

We all have had these moments. And if you haven't, just wait. It's coming.

> A time is coming when you will run out of creativity,
> When you will run out of health,
> When you will run out of contacts and networks,
> When you will run out of money
> When you will run out of whatever it is that you think has *gotten you this* far in life.

And, you will need for God to show up in your life with power and authority. You will need to seek God with all you've got inside of you. You may even need to say, "my God, I don't know what to do."

The text teaches that these situations, these "my hands are tied and I don't know what to do" situations are best handled by going to God in prayer. Jehoshaphat had gotten some bad news. He and all of the people under his reign were in danger. But, he did not give into the anxiety. He was not dismayed. The text says that "he set himself to seek the Lord." He called a corporate fast. He called the people together to pray and lead them in an epic prayer.

2. He prayed a prayer that recalls that God reigns.

In verse three, we see that although he was "alarmed," the king made up his mind that he would "inquire of the Lord." And, when he began to pray, he said, "Lord, the God of our ancestors, are you not the God who is in heaven? Do you not rule over all of the nations? In your hand are power and might, so that no one can withstand you."

He is recalling that God reigns, and that God is in control of all things. He goes on to say, "Did you not drive out the inhabitants of this land and give it to us to inhabit?" In other words, "Not only are you powerful and in control now, but you *have been* in the past. You've always been in control. You've always had all the power. And in the past, you've used your dominion and your power to do some mighty things on our behalf."

I don't know about you, but when I face difficulties in life and I can't see how things will work out, it helps me, it ministers to me, and it encourages me to think about how God has intervened on my behalf before. It helps me to recall the times that God has rescued me and replay the instances in which God certainly saved my life. Because of God's impressive track record in my life, my faith is lifted and I become convinced—all over again—that God is still able. God is still on the throne. As God was in the beginning, is now and ever shall be, our God is sovereign!

This word comes to us today to encourage those that believe that their situation is beyond help, and to convict somebody who thinks even for a second that your power compares to God's power and that your plan is smarter than God's plan. God is the One who is running this show! It's a good thing that God is, and we are not!

When we are in prayer, we must also remind God of the promises that God has made. It's *not* that God has forgotten, but sometimes, you have to pray to remind yourself that this thing will not end until God's Word has come to pass! The king prayed, "Did you not give this land forever to the descendants of your friend Abraham?" In other words, "God, let us remind you that you made us a promise. Surely, if this attack were to take place today, and were to succeed, it would be contrary to what You've already said!"

In other words, "*we know that, because You are not a God that You should lie, nor are You the Son of Man that you should repent, that this can't be how this story is going to end. Because no word from You shall return to us void. This thing can't be over now. Because You watch over your Word to see that it is fulfilled. So, watch over us now, God, and see to it that your people are not destroyed!*"

To each of us, God has spoken things that cannot be reversed. God has made promises that will not be broken. You see, God isn't like us. God does what God says God is going to do. Psalm 138 teaches us that the only thing that God puts above God's name is God's Word. Therefore, you can't be dismayed by what you see right now, *if what you see is not what God said.*

> You might feel like the underdog, but God called you the "head and not the tail."
> You might feel like no one sees you or understands you, but God calls you "the apple of God's eye."
> You might be feeling as if you're under siege, but God promised, "He would give His angels charge over you to keep you in all of your ways."

Can you get excited about God's Word? Can you get excited that God keeps God's word? You may need to pray and remind God that you know what that God said:

Are you sick? Then remind God, "You said, by your stripes, I am healed."

Are you sad? Then remind God, "You said, that the joy of the Lord would be my strength!"

Feel ambushed by life? Then remind God "You said, that when the enemy shall come in like a flood, then you would lift up a standard against him!"

3. Finally, he relinquished his control over the situation.

"We have no power to face this vast army that is attacking us. *We don't know what to do, but our eyes are on you.*" I know that that is a troubling thought to many of us who like to be in control, or to think that we are in control. Those of us who like to have a plan, and like for our plans to work every single time. But, what do you do when what is ahead of you is unknown? What do you do when you can't see what's around the corner? How do you plan for that?

How do you plan when everything you've worked for, and even your very life, are now in danger of destruction? When it seems as if your hopes and dreams aren't unfolding as you'd like and you can't see exactly how to move forward?

I will never forget how stressed and afraid I was throughout my last year of seminary. Everyone around me was either getting jobs or getting into doctoral programs, and I didn't have any options coming to me. As much as I tried to remain hopeful, I had to confide in my mother, "I am so stressed about my future."

Astonished, my mother replied, "after all the work you've done and how you've given your life to God for His service, why are you afraid that He won't take care of you? If I were you, *I would get excited about how God is about to bless you.*"

I realize now that I was so stressed out because *I* did not know what was ahead of me, and *I* did not know what to do. I know that it is troubling to many of us to have to say this, but sometimes, it is simply the truth to say, "I just don't know what to do." When it seems as if you've tried everything you know to do and none of it is working. When you've given it all you've got and nothing fruitful is coming to fruition. Sometimes, you just have to face the fact, and state the fact, that "I just don't know what to do."

Here is a word of hope to those of you who are stuck somewhere, "and you just don't know what to do."

> When you finally give up on all of your ingenious ideas,
> When you finally get tired of banging your head against the proverbial wall,
> When you finally get tired of your children not acting right,
> When you finally get tired of your dating life not going right,
> When you finally get tired of your money being funny and your change being strange, and,
> When you see that if you were to lay your hands on this situation, it would be worse than it already is,

We serve a God who stands ready to work God's perfect plan. God has a way of seeing things for what they are, from the beginning to the end, and every detail in between. God sees what you're facing, and God is ready, willing, and able to do what you need God to do. *God is simply waiting on you to step back, let go, and let God.* Take your hands off of the situation you are facing. Stop trying to manipulate it to your benefit.

Jehoshaphat could have taken this matter into his own hands and advanced, or just sat waiting to be destroyed. But, he said a powerful prayer: "We don't know what to do, but our eyes are on you." That's a powerful prayer. Why? Because he shifted the focus from him and his limited power to the great and mighty—can't fail—power of God.

That is the time *to get excited*! When you have given it over to God, you should get excited! When you can take your eyes off of the situation and put them on God, you should get excited at what God is about to do. "We don't know what to do," prayed the king, "but our eyes are on you!"

More than eighty years ago, Zora Neal Hurston penned the majestic book, *Their Eyes Were Watching God*. This book has seen me through many seasons and has answered many questions. In the opening lines of the book, she writes of the people of Eatonville,

Florida, "they seemed to be staring at the dark, but their eyes were watching God." Hurston suggests that we all have a choice of where we fix our eyes and focus our gaze. Hurston asks us from eternity, *are your eyes still watching God?*

Another king, David, put it like this: "I lift up my eyes to the hills! Where does my help come from? My help comes from the Lord," the Maker of heaven and earth. He will not let your foot slip; He who watches over you will not slumber!" God is watching over you. If you can suspend your fear long enough to just put your eyes on God, it is time to get excited. It's time to get excited!

When you're excited, you give up your right to worry. You give up your tendency to fear or become anxious, as *if God is not in control.*

Get excited! Because when God steps in, God works things out for your good. King J. recalled that God reigns, reminded God of God's promises, and relinquished his own control, thereby setting himself up for an incredible victory. I'm wondering if there may be one or two, who, like me, can't see everything clearly, but can get excited that God *is going* to move?

I can get excited because of what I can see in my spirit, because I believe that my God is able to do anything but fail. I get excited because God is moving some things around on my behalf and God is in the background putting some things in place just for me.

If you see me walking with a little more pep in my step, know that I'm excited. I don't always know what's ahead of me. But, my eyes are watching God and I believe that great things are in store for me.

> Despite the rain clouds above my head. I'm excited.
> Despite the conditions in the Church. I'm excited.
> Despite the battles that are before me. I'm excited.

Are your eyes on God? Then, let's praise God in advance for the victory. Maybe wave your hand and throw your head back and say, "Yes God! My eyes are on You and I'm excited!"

WHAT I KNOW FOR SURE

ROMANS 8:35, 38-39 (NRSV)

Preached August 2015, Trinity UCC, Chicago, IL.

One thing I know for sure is that "the only constant thing in our lives is change." Change, my brothers and sisters, is just a part of life.
   From the growth of a child into an adult,
      to the transition of Summer into Autumn, into Winter into Spring,
   from the planting of a seed to the blossoming and flourishing of a flower,
   to the beautiful dance from the womb to the tomb,
   change is always happening.

   Change happens whether we invite it or not. It can happen on a scale so large that we can't overlook it, or it can happen in spurts so small that we hardly recognize that it's taking place.
   Change can occur slowly, gingerly, leisurely, running a slow course over time, or change can come like a thief in the night, so fast, so fleeting, so surprising.
   Change has a mind of its own. It decides what it wants to do, how it will impact our lives, what emotions it will call forth, what condition it will leave us in.

   Some change is positive.
      It's necessary.

It's refreshing and surprising in the best way.

It's the dead weight you lay down after years of being burdened.

It's the deliverance from addiction and the healing from affliction.

It's the birth of new seasons, new ideas, new relationships, new children.

It's the coming of the sun after months of frigid cold and gloom.

Some change is not so positive. It can be surprising in the worst of ways.

The sudden loss of life,

The relapse into addiction or sickness,

The heart that is broken from life's unapologetic twists and turns, or

The situation so stubborn and so difficult that it simply doesn't seem to change.

Change is a part of living. I don't care who you are; I don't care what you do for a living or where you acquired your degrees; I don't care who you know or what your last name is, you've got a question to answer today: *what will you do when change comes?*

What is your plan for when change comes knocking at your door? How will you respond? Will you open your arms and embrace what God is doing? I know it's not the prayer of every heart in the sanctuary because it's such a hard prayer to pray, but will you pray the prayer of Jesus, "not my will but yours be done?" Or, will you resist the move of God? Will you tell God, "not now, now is not the time. I don't have what it takes to withstand this change." *What will you do?*

Since change is always on the cusp of our lives, always on the horizon, it will help you to know what you're going to do when the winds of change begin to blow; when the waves of transition begin to rage; when you are visited by an abrupt about-face; or when the subtleties of life's switches inch their way into your atmosphere. Do you know for sure what you will do?

So, again, the question arises, what do you *know* for sure that will hold you when change inevitably comes? What do you *know* for certain that will keep you grounded when the ground is crumbling beneath your feet? What do you *know*, for real *know*? *What is your conviction* in the midst of transition? The text gives us answers:

1. You must know who God is to you.

We should pause here to say that despite its placement in the New Testament, the book of Romans is largely considered Paul's last will and testament. It is basically his final reflection and summary of the Gospel, and how the Gospel has been activated in his life and beyond. That being said, at the time of writing, Paul has been through some things. He has been through some hard afflictions, and some faulty convictions. He has been arrested, imprisoned, and exiled. He has planted churches, raised up pastors, and suffered for the sake of Christ. On one hand, we know this. On the other hand, we know that it was his faith and his confession that *nothing* could separate him from the love of Christ.

He goes on to show that after some time of walking with God, after so many times of seeing God work things out on your behalf, after seeing God and feeling God move things around for you, you ought to have a constant confession that nothing can separate you from the love of God, through Christ Jesus.

In the course of change, knowing and believing God to be your Provider will hold you when the ends aren't meeting and the money isn't stretching out long enough.

In the course of change, knowing and believing God to be your Healer will hold you in times of infirmity or weakness.

In the course of change, knowing and believing God to be your Peace will hold you when chaos and confusion break out all around you.

Knowing and believing God to be your Banner on the Battlefield will hold you when you feel as if your life is in danger.

Who is God to you?
Who do you *know* your God to be?

Who do you *believe* your God to be?

I say to you that you must be clear about who your God is to you when changes come your way. This is what I know for sure!

2. You have to know who you are in God.

What else do I know for sure? There's this strange side effect of change that will have you thinking that you don't know what you know. It has a confusing and discombobulating effect that can leave your head spinning, causing you to wonder, "What just happened here?" How interesting it is that life can happen, and all of sudden, it can leave you disheveled and hurting, with a skewered sense of who you are. I know that feeling. In fact, I think that many of us know this feeling. Why? Because to be Black in America is to live in a state of constant confusion. It is to live in the dark—both proverbially and literally. It is to live in a drama that is infested with death-dealing mystery. It is to live in the constant confusion that comes from unanswered questions. Questions, such as:

> How does an ebullient, beautiful and intelligent woman like Sandra Bland, go from landing her dream job at her alma mater to "committing suicide" in a Texas jail cell? Why was she *really* pulled over, and why did her routine traffic stop eventually lead to her arrest? Why not a ticket and a court date? Why is the man who opened up her car door and told her, "I will light you up" still gainfully employed in Texas?

Questions, such as what really happened to Michael Brown? What really happened to Tanisha Anderson? What really happened to Renisha McBride? And, why is there no consequence or repercussion for the stealing of their lives? I don't know about you, but questions such as these inevitably lead to questions like, "Am I next? Is my brother or my father or my mother or my sister next? My niece or my nephew?"

These questions lead to other questions, such as "Why do we have to teach Black people to be scared of cops, when we should be teaching cops not to kill Black people?"

Something is wrong with these changes that we're going through as a people. Something is scary about these changes. There's no way that we can walk with our heads held high when we feel that our heads are moving targets for the next stray bullet from a police officer's gun.

How do you live and walk in the confidence of the Word that tells us that we are sons and daughters of God when we have to demand and insist that our lives matter?

How can we sing the songs of the Lord in this strange land, where to survive means having to shuck and jive, and to live can mean living in fear for your life?

These changes are confusing. The conditions we are facing lie in stark contrast to the word of God that tells us that we are, "a royal priesthood and a holy nation." Meanwhile, so many *false prophets* want to offer cheap theological consolation and suggest that dying in this way was "God's plan" for someone's life. I struggle with that because that is incompatible with the theology of the Jesus Christ that we serve, who said that He came that we'd have *life* and life *more abundantly*. We serve the God who said, "I know the plans that I have towards you, plans to prosper you and not to harm you. To give you hope and a future."

God clearly believes in us and has things in mind for us to do. I believe that, when a Black man, woman, boy or girl is unjustly killed, it's actually an interruption of God's plan and that God's heart is broken by the loss of another precious life. I believe that God has to get going with "plan B," trying to figure out who will accomplish what the fallen was destined to accomplish in this world. It's not God's plan for kids to get shot in parks or on their bicycles. It wasn't God's plan for Eric Garner to be suffocated while he was trying to make his ends meet, or for Sandra to die in a dark and dismal jail cell just for standing up for herself.

Subsequently, it's not God's plan that these circumstances should make us shirk from our Godly identity. I know this for sure, because the text says that "in all these things we are more than conquerors though Him who loved us."

Paul goes on to say that, "I am convinced that neither death, nor life, nor angel, rulers, things present, things to come, powers, height nor death, nor anything in else in all creation will be able to separate us from God's love." Therefore, it is clear that change will come, and our lives are susceptible and vulnerable to all kinds of changes, including death, apparently, even untimely and unjust deaths. Here, in the case of Paul, his hope wasn't in himself, but in the promises of God that sustained him through it all.

If your idea of who you are is hinged upon your success or by what others think about you, you're standing on shaky ground. However, if you draw your strength and your self-esteem and your security from the promises of God, you will be able to stand with conviction through whatever you face. Paul is clear. Hardship will come. Distress or persecution or fame or nakedness or peril or sword may come. But even in the time of changes such as these, the promise is that we are still conquerors. No, we are not conquerors because we're so strong and so determined. Rather, we are conquerors because we are richly and extravagantly loved by Jesus!

We are still sons and daughters of the Most High. We are still hidden under the shadow of the Almighty. When you begin to know these promises, and know that they can't be changed, and know that they will be fulfilled; you have to walk differently in the world. You have to carry yourself with confidence and keep on letting fear go. I know for sure that I am a conqueror because God sustains me.

3. If you have the faith, God has the power.

Obviously, there are some challenges and some changes implied in the text. And obviously, we can't look to or cling to external things for our continuity and security because everything must change. Your faith must be in something unchangeable. The songwriter said it like this: "Time is filled with swift transition, naught on earth unmoved can stand. Build your hope on things eternal. Hold to God's unchanging hand."

I learned this hymn and many others as a young girl in Texas, at New Lincoln Missionary Baptist Church, where up until last year, Rev. Alvin Evans, Sr., my grandfather, served as pastor for more than forty years. This man would end every sermon with one question, "Ain't he alright?" This man let me preach in his pulpit when no one else would, and offered to license me to preach after hearing me preach one time.

Several weeks ago, I rushed home to be with my grandfather as he crossed his finish line into eternity. For about ten days, I watched someone, who knew his God, leave this world behind. I watched and I listened. I saw that even though he was dependent on an oxygen mask, every now and then he would start talking about Jesus and become so filled with the Spirit, that he would have us remove his mask so he could talk more freely. He'd get a miraculous second wind every time he'd talk about Jesus, and he talked about Jesus to everyone who entered the room. To every nurse, he'd ask, "Do you know the Lord?" To every doctor, he'd say, "Have you been water baptized?" They would just let him talk, until he got all of his witnessing and evangelizing out of his belly.

I had many conversations with him. One in particular I had to remember because he made me make him a promise. He said, "Wherever you go and wherever you preach, tell the people of God this: *if you have the faith, God has the power*. Don't add to it, don't change it." I asked him to elaborate as much as he could. "It doesn't take grace or strength or anything else for God to move His hand in our lives. It only takes faith. If you have the faith that God can do anything, God will do whatever you need God to do."

I'm here today, a messenger of God and Pastor Evans, to declare *one more thing* that I know for sure:

> In the midst of your change, if you have the faith, God has the power!
> If you have the faith, God has the power.
> If you have the faith to stand, God has the power to sustain you.
> If you have the faith to keep on living, God has the power to hold you up.
> If you have the faith to pray, God has the power to answer.
> If you have the faith to get up, God has the power to keep you up and let you soar.
> If you have the faith to endure the hardship, God has the power to bring you through.

If you have the faith to believe that you're more than a conqueror, God has the power to show you that there's nothing that you can't overcome.

It's good news that God's power doesn't rely on your ability, your worthiness, your deservingness, your intelligence, your beauty, or your connections. God doesn't need any of that. *All* God needs is your faith. God needs you to believe that God is who God said God is, and that God will do just what God said.

I know for sure, that if you have the faith, God will show you God's power. Believe me when I tell you, *God has got power.*

The wind and waves must obey God's command, because God's got power.
The arc of time bends to accommodate God's plans and purposes, because God's got power.
The earth is God's footstool and heaven is God's throne, because God has got power.
There is deliverance in God's Word and healing in God's touch, because God has got power.
God's presence is constant, and God's love is unchanging, from generation to generation!
God's got power!

God opens blinded eyes to see.
God releases stammering tongues to speak.
God fixes the broken and restores the weak.
God redeems the sinner and reclaims the lost.
God raises the dead from their graves.

And, God doesn't need our advice. God doesn't need our input or consultation. God doesn't need our intervention or our opinion. God doesn't need my direction or your direction, and he surely don't need any help, because God's got the power all by God's Self.

I know it! I know for sure, that God's got this! God's got me. God's got you.

God is in control of every change and every circumstance.

And I'm so glad that God promised, in this very same chapter, that all things work together . . . All things work together . . . All things work together . . . ALL things work together for our good. And when they work for our good, they work for God's glory.

Who knows that when it works out for our good, it's also for God's glory? Is there anyone willing to give God glory? Glory for God's goodness! Glory for God's kindness! Glory for his faithfulness!

Give the Lord some glory!

ABOUT THE AUTHOR

Rev. Neichelle R. Guidry is a spiritual daughter of New Creation Christian Fellowship of San Antonio, Texas, where the Bishop David Michael Copeland and the Rev. Dr. Claudette Anderson Copeland are her pastors and where she was ordained to ministry in 2010. She is a graduate of Clark Atlanta University (2007, BA, Lambda Pi Eta) and Yale Divinity School (2010, M.Div.), where she was the 2010 recipient of the Walcott Prize for Clear and Effective Public and Pulpit Speaking. Currently, she serves as the Liaison to Worship and Arts Ministries in the Office of the Senior Pastor at Trinity United Church of Christ on the South side of Chicago, where the Rev. Dr. Otis Moss, III is the Senior Pastor. She is the creator of *shepreaches*, a virtual community and professional development organization that aspires to uplift African-American millennial women in ministry through theological reflection, fellowship, and liturgical curation. Neichelle is a Doctor of Philosophy candidate in Liturgical Studies (Homiletics) at Garrett-Evangelical Theological Seminary in Evanston, Illinois. She was recently listed as one of "12 New Faces of Black Leadership" in *TIME* Magazine (January 2015). She was recognized for "quickly becoming one of her generation's most powerful female faith leaders" on Ebony Magazine's 2015 Power 100 list (December 2015). Additionally, Rev. Neichelle and the work of *shepreaches* were featured in the *New York Times* (April 3, 2015). She is a contributor to *What Would Jesus Ask? Christian Leaders Reflect on His Questions of Faith* (Time Books, 2015), and the author of the forthcoming book, Curating a World: Words from a Young Woman Who Preaches (MMGI Books, April 2016).

"In 2013, "Rev. N" was invited to preach the opening worship service of the United Church of Christ's biennial General Synod. Concurrently, she became one of twenty-two contributors to *Those Sisters Can Preach! 22 Pearls of Wisdom, Virtue and Hope* (Pilgrim Press, 2013), a compilation of sermons written by members of Delta Sigma Theta Sorority, Incorporated, in honor of the Sorority's Centennial Anniversary. Bishop Vashti Murphy McKenzie, the Sorority's National Chaplain, edited the volume. Additionally, the EnVest Foundation recognized her as a "Top 40 Under 40" Award Recipient in 2013. Neichelle is a 2013 Beatitudes Society Fellow, and a Fellow of the Inaugural Black Theology and Leadership Institute at Princeton Theological Seminary.